Winter Music

A Life of Jessica Powers: Poet, Nun, Woman of the 20th Century

Dolores R. Leckey

Sheed & Ward

Sheed & Ward™ is a service of The National Catholic Reporter Publishing Company.

Library of Congress Cataloguing-in-Publication Data

Leckey, Dolores R.,

Winter music : a life of Jessica Powers : poet, nun, woman of the 20th century / Dolores R. Leckey.

p. cm.

Includes bibliographical references and index.

ISBN 1-55612-559-3 (alk. paper)

1. Powers, Jessica--Biography. 2. Poets, American--20th century--Biography. 3. Carmelite Nuns--United States--Biography I. Title.

PS3531.09723Z75 1992

811′.54--dc20 92-27486

[B] CIP

Published by: Sheed & Ward
115 E. Armour Blvd.
P.O. Box 419492
Kansas City, MO 64141-6492

To order, call: (800) 333-7373

Cover illustration and design by Gloria Ortiz.

Contents

Acknowledgements

For six years I have worked on this life of Jessica Powers. During that time I have not been alone; many have labored with me. In the forefront of these co-laborers are Bishop Robert Morneau and Father Bernard McGarty.

It was Bishop Morneau who introduced me to the poetry of Jessica Powers, for me a life-changing introduction. Father McGarty, her cousin, himself a journalist, wrote an article about her that opened a window onto a fascinating, complex and profound human being. Because of them I began this project while Jessica Powers was yet alive, and with them I continued the work after her death. I could not have labored without them.

The men and women of Cat Tail Valley, friends and relatives of Jessica Powers, are important contributors to the book. A few months after Jessica Powers's funeral, they gathered in Mauston's St. Patrick's rectory to share with me their memories, their knowledge, their laughter and tears. I am deeply grateful to all of them for their interest in and support of the book. William and Mary Walsh have provided me with facts and photos; they carefully read and corrected the Wisconsin portion where needed. They are natural historians who love their land and their people. William Walsh's memory and capacity for detail were a source of security for me. Doris Trainer Scully, a first cousin of Jessica, generously responded to my requests for information about the Trainer family. Another cousin, Rev. Daniel Morrissey, O.P. in a lengthy interview provided valuable family background. He also loaned me his personal copies of *The Lantern Burns* and *The Place of Splendor*. Other relatives—Father Bede Jogue, O.P. and Maureen Powers—shared correspondence.

Sister Eileen Surles, a Religious of the Cenacle, who was with Jessica Powers in New York, read that section for accuracy. She relived for me scenes and feelings, calling forth from memory the stories of Jessica's years in New York City.

Carmelite Sisters welcomed me into their monasteries so I could learn more about them and so learn more about Jessica. The sisters in Elysburg, Pennsylvania had preserved Jessica's letters to Christopher Powell—how the letters came to the monastery in Elysburg is a story in itself. These letters were important in understanding the young Jessica Powers.

In San Diego I had the privilege of long conversations with Sister Desiree, a close friend of Jessica's; and in the Philadelphia carmel Sister Magdalene shared memories of her extraordinary grandfather, Clifford Laube. She also connected me with her parents, John and Genevieve Tully, who were interviewed for the book. Sister Constance Fitzgerald of the Baltimore monastery allowed me into the archives, and was available for consultation. All of these carmels provided valuable assistance. Most especially I thank the sisters of the Mother of God Carmel in Pewaukee, Wisconsin who over and over again went the extra mile for me, providing papers (journals, letters, scrapbooks) and prayers. They painstakingly read and commented on Part Three—Carmel—as did Teresa Hahn formerly of the Pewaukee community. Any errors, either of fact or emphasis, are mine not theirs. Through these contacts I have come to value the treasure of Carmelite spirituality more than ever. Special thanks to the Laube family and to Tom Coffey, whom the Laube family named to manage the Monastine Press after the death of Clifford Laube.

Five people read the entire manuscript, and their critique significantly shaped the text. Dana Greene, historian and biographer, asked me needed hard questions during the preparatory stage and especially when at last there was a text. Thomas J. Leckey, also brought a historian's perspective to the text, and Sister Gretchen Dysart, a video producer, assessed the book from an artistic viewpoint. Bishop Morneau and Father McGarty read with editors' eyes. The book's virtues are enhanced because of these readers; the book's faults are my own.

Charles Elston and John LeDoux of Marquette University, were unfailingly courteous in helping me navigate the university archives. Sister Regina Siegfried, A.S.C., one of the editors of *Selected Poetry of Jessica Powers*, had organized Jessica Powers's poems chronologically, and this made my work much easier. Bonnie Stallings typed the manuscript with skill and remarkable patience. She accepted the constant changes with grace and good humor.

The Washington Biography group with whom I met regularly while the book was in preparation provided insight, challenge, encouragement and practical suggestions. In particular, Marc Pachter, the convener, through his own deep love of biography, inspired me to walk down unfamiliar writing pathways.

All of these are my collaborators. Together we have created *Winter Music*, and to each one I am deeply appreciative. There is one more. Jessica Powers. Certainly before her death she was actively engaged in the work. Since then she has seemed to me a steady presence, close at hand, close to heart, especially so when my gaze lingers on the cattails I gathered from the valley of her childhood.

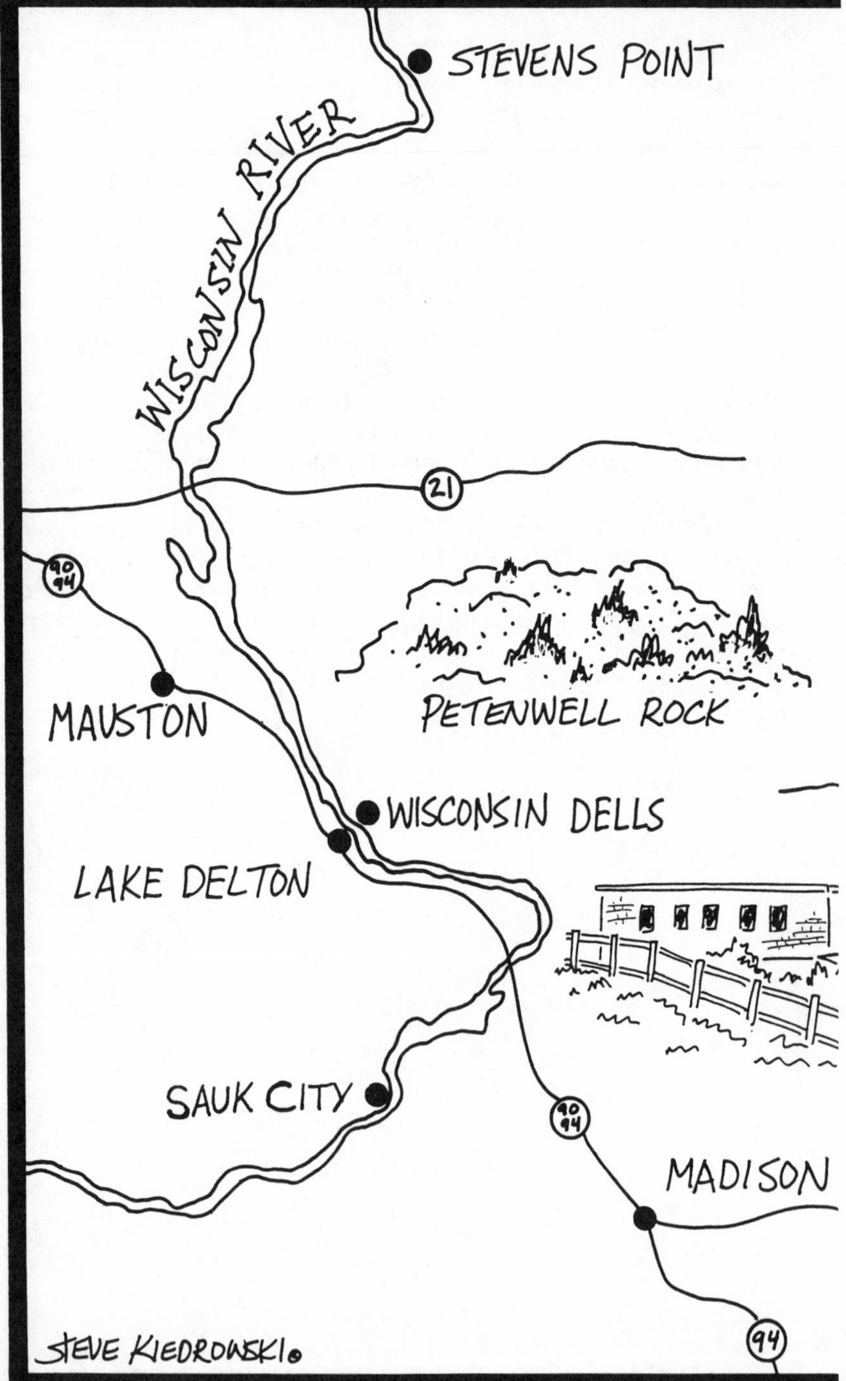

STEVENS POINT
WISCONSIN RIVER
21
90
94
MAUSTON
PETENWELL ROCK
WISCONSIN DELLS
LAKE DELTON
SAUK CITY
90
94
MADISON
94
STEVE KIEDROWSKI©

ST. PATRICK'S
CARMELITE MONASTERY
MADISON
94
MILWAUKEE
PEWAUKEE
94

Dedicated
to the memory
of my parents

Prelude

I sat alone in the work room of the Carmelite monastery, waiting, not really expecting her to appear. It was nine o'clock on a hot July evening in 1988. The monastery was silent except for crickets' songs that entered through the open windows.

Then I heard her footsteps, light as a child's, padding down the corridor. In a moment she was there, a small woman dressed in the brown habit and black veil of the ancient order of Carmelites. She was tired after the day's editing session, readying her new book, *Selected Poetry of Jessica Powers*, for publication. Her age (eighty-three), her fragile health, her fatigue—it was all there in her face. So was a certain eagerness. She had come with a purpose: she wanted to talk.

I often think about that night when she spoke of many things. It was as if she deliberately opened a door, and through the passage way were clues about the woman whose exquisite lyrics had touched so many people for more than half a century. I had begun work on her biography two years earlier, drawn to her first by her poetry, and then by the bare outline of her life. I wanted to know more. That night she mapped for me what routes I should follow. Six weeks later she was dead.

> My soul is out on paths that have no ending
> and no return. A light blurs out my way.
> I am with God and toward my godhead tending.
> I near the foothills of eternal day
>
> O far
>
> O far away.
>
> God speaks to me. Earth has no more to say.
> ("The Song of Distance," 84)[1]

The facts of Jessica Powers's life can be arranged in three parts. She spent the first thirty-one years of her life on a farm in Mauston, Wisconsin, except for a brief period at Marquette University's School of Journalism, and another in Chicago, Illinois. She wrote over a hundred serious poems during this time, most of them published in newspapers, magazines, and poetry journals. In 1936 she went to New York to be closer to the pulse of the literary world and to the Catholic Revival centered (in the United States) in New York. There she published her first volume of poetry, *The Lantern Burns* (1939). She was able to support herself by her writing, possible because she lived with friends and had few wants or needs—only God and literature.

In 1941, she abruptly left her circle of writer friends and her burgeoning career to enter the Carmelite cloister in Milwaukee, one of the most rigorous religious orders in the Catholic Church. She was prepared to relinquish that which was dearest to her, her "songs," as she liked to refer to her poems. That didn't happen. She was given permission to continue her writing, and in the course of forty-seven years she published hundreds of new poems, including four books, *The Place of Splendor* (1946), *Mountain Sparrow* (1972), *Journey to Bethlehem* (1980), and *The House at Rest* (1984), and a children's book, *The Little Alphabet* (1955). Six weeks before her death she was still working with the editors of a new collection, her largest, reviewing each and every poem that was to be included in *Selected Poetry of Jessica Powers.* This, then, is the outline of where she lived and what she accomplished, a bare sketch of her life. This biography, *Winter Music*, is an attempt to add detail and color to the picture, to show the richness of a life lived from a creative center.

I have organized her story in three parts, corresponding with the landscapes of her life. Of the twelve chapters, however, six deal with her Wisconsin years. Wisconsin was the foundation of her entire life, formative in several ways. By that I mean she came into the world the grandchild of pioneers. Two sets of grandparents settled the Cat Tail Valley area of Wisconsin and she carried their genes, complete with the complementary desires to seek new frontiers and to "settle," to create a home and *to be* at home. The geography of

Wisconsin, the spaces, the bluffs, the marshes, the birds and especially the weather shaped her stance in the world. "I came to birth here in a month of snows,/ and it is only winter my mind knows—," she wrote in "The House of the Silver Spirit" (125). Winter in all its forms, spiritual, emotional, intellectual as well as meteorological, runs through her writing. She learned to live sparely, esthetically, deliberately, daringly, deeply in Wisconsin. It was winter that vibrated through her being, like music. "Music filled me so much I couldn't bear it," she told me. Wisconsin trained her eye so that her contemplative gaze became the way she looked out upon the world. Wisconsin taught her about adversity and encouraged her adventuresome spirit. It was there she began to create her own winter music.

She went to New York in search of an artistic and spiritual center, she said, but something of Wisconsin was always with her. New York did not frighten her, a young woman from a farming community, unsophisticated but eager for experience. She was energized by the people, by the pace, by the books, by her work. Her adventuresome spirit "reveled" in the city. There she learned needed technical disciplines; she learned the boundaries of her music. All of this was enormously important to her, but still, the well of loneliness was ever present, a longing that could not be satisfied, not even by occasional sojourns in Wisconsin, not even by the joy of her first book. She was "a milkweed seed/ anchored securely to a wisp of down." Until Carmel.

> There is a garden: pray the wind may let
> Her down in that soil where her roots can move.
> Ask God to hold her, till her roots are set
> Safe in the windless moment of His love.[2]

A religious community could offer her a place of stability and growth, where her contemplative nature could be at home. In 1941 there were many different groups of contemplatives in the United States. Why, then Carmel? Why so severe a way of life, enclosed and apart, penitential and rigorous?

Jessica Powers had a capacity for the difficult and, in fact, given a range of choices, she tended toward the more difficult. She was in the tradition of Rainer Maria Rilke who wrote,

> . . . It is clear that we must hold to what is difficult; everything alive holds to it, everything in Nature grows and defends itself in its own way and is characteristically and spontaneously itself, seeks at all costs to be so and against all opposition. We know little, but that we must hold to what is difficult is a certainty that will not forsake us; . . . that something is difficult must be a reason the more for us to do it.[3]

Like Rilke, the difficult choice was the natural choice for her. But I think there was another reason, one grounded in Catholic theology.

In 1941, as Hitler's aggression was fast becoming a world war, and evil seemed to be in the ascendancy, as suffering was imposed on innocent people, here and there men and women of God took a stand. They hid Jewish refugees or organized schools for children in concentration camps; they comforted the dying and guarded human dignity. Some of them, a world away from the actual battles and bombs, chose a stance of solidarity with the suffering. Through prayer, voluntary penance and personal sacrifice they gave themselves to God for God's purposes. Thomas Merton entered a Trappist monastery; Jessica Powers became a Carmelite. In that period of worldwide turmoil cloisters were full. "The Little Nation," first published in 1940 in *The Washington Post* is revealing of Jessica Powers's central motivation.

> Having no gift of strategy or arms,
> no secret weapon and no walled defense,
> I shall become a citizen of love,
> that little nation with the blood-stained sod
> where even the slain have power, the only country
> that sends forth an ambassador to God.
>
> Renouncing self and crying out to evil
> to end its wars, I seek a land that lies
> all unprotected like a sleeping child;
> nor is my journey reckless and unwise.
> Who doubts that love has an effective weapon
> may meet with a surprise.[4]

Carmel was where she took her stand against evil, armed with the daily practice of sacrificial love.

There was one more reason. She knew she needed a strong structure, "lest I dream myself away," she said. The monastery, with its daily schedule of eighteen accountable hours, left little time for dreaming. It was for her the place to settle her pioneer soul with hard work and alertness, the qualities her ancestors brought to Wisconsin.

Clearly, Carmel was a liminal experience in the life of Jessica Powers. Yet, I devote only three chapters to these forty-seven years. There is much about the inner workings of a Carmelite monastery, the seismic changes that occurred in Carmelite life before, during and after the Second Vatican Council, and the creative political movements within this most unique of subcultures that I am not competent to relate. These factors are all important pieces of the context in which Jessica Powers lived and wrote. Still, I believe that Jessica Powers, the poet, the contemplative nun, the woman of the twentieth century, lived to some degree on the edges of the context. Carmelite renewal profoundly affected her community life. But my reading of her life is that these conflicts and tensions and often serious troubles were transformed into a sharpened and confirmed awareness of that which she had already known: death is the central reality of life, usually banished to the margins by most of us, but requiring a necessary rapprochement if ultimately we are to have a whole and healthy life. She made that rapprochement. She knew the hard beauties of winter.

I have not related all the details of the life of Jessica Powers. Not only would that be impossible, it would not serve her artistic and spiritual vision which always pointed to larger, universal realities. My goal has been "to spin a mood, not to hold the note" as Willa Cather once wrote[5]; to touch on something and then pass on.

Neither have I attempted to analyze her poetry, either from a literary or a theological perspective. I have tried to tell her story, or more accurately, to let her tell her story through the medium of her poetry, for that is what she did. Her poems, totally uncontrived, sprang from her life, her life within and the external conditions of her personal world, and the larger world in which she dwelt. She worked her poems, of course. She revised, and rewrote. But one can trace her story line in the music she created. Even the poems that are more didactic (and so more prose than poetry), the result perhaps of the tension between revelation and explanation, reflect a particular point in the unfolding of her life.

But why tell this particular life? What is there about Jessica Powers that can have meaning for people in these last years of the twentieth century?

In the Marquette University archives, which now house the Jessica Powers papers, are letters from around the world that partially answer that question. A nun from Australia writes how much it meant to see her photo on the 1984 collection, *The House at Rest*, to see that she had made it "to a ripe age through a life that, judging from your poems, had much inner pain and oscillation toward God." And from Italy, "I guess you had romantic feelings in your youth which must surely have influenced your love for nature and its creatures." And another, from California, "It (your poetry) is like listening to your heart." There are hundreds of such letters, from every continent, from people in all walks of life. Not academicians, nor educators, but searching people, touched by Jessica Powers's art, people who found that poetry mattered to them.

Her poetry continues to affect people at the core of their lives. Tilden Edwards, an Episcopal priest, director of the Shalem Institute for Spiritual Formation, uses her poetry in his daily prayer. "I feel absolutely understood by her," he says. The London Grail has used *The House at Rest* in conferences and retreats. Her work has inspired at least one new book of meditations that combines fifteen of her poems with the writings of others (Thomas Merton, for example), line drawings and lines of music.[6] One doctoral dissertation on her spirituality is now completed and another is in progress.[7] A variety of journals, from spiritual life to rural life, have featured her poetry since her death. She and the people of society, ordinary people, continue a vital connection, soul to soul.

I answer the question this way. The fact of her poetry, the way she crafted language, is reason to tell her story. Her words are simple, unadorned, direct, surprising and spacious. They are bearers of truth, beauty and love expressed without pretension or manipulation. She respected language and refused to violate it, rejecting what she sensed was a growing cynicism in poetry. Who does not long for a return to clear and unambiguous public discourse?[8] Jessica Powers, who has been compared to Emily Dickinson and linked with the Carmelite mystical poet, John of the Cross, is a lamp along that path.[9]

She sought beauty, and her music's purpose was to convey her discoveries which pointed to other, more subtle beauty. The times hunger for true beauty, not for imitations. Some among us believe that beauty can be a catalyst for positive change. For example, Nobel scientist Konrad Lorenz has argued that it may be possible *through beauty* to inspire overworked people who are alienated from nature with a sense of what is good and of their duty to protect and preserve nature's living things.[10] At the very least Jessica Powers's nature poetry can be an abiding inspiration for what must surely be an ongoing national commitment to ecology.

Perhaps the most important reason for narrating this life is what we can learn about suffering. She knew about suffering in its many forms. She knew about it in her teens, in her twenties, in her thirties—in fact, throughout the course of her entire life. And she learned how to transform it into something of exquisite value. Ours is a time of deep depression and struggle for many people of all ages. Jessica Powers's experience can be instructive and inspiring.

Jessica Powers would never have called herself a feminist. But as she tells her story, creatively and honestly, through her poems, in the different stages of womanhood—even into old age—one senses a mentor in the meters and the rhymes. She shows us how creativity can deepen in elderhood if we remain engaged with others, with our heart's work, and with the continuing call of God in our lives. Women have learned, in this last generation, that there is power in our shared stories. In Jessica Powers's life and work we touch her gentle power, which flowed from the God she loved so passionately, the source of her winter music. That touch enables us to understand something of our own possibilities.

Part One

WISCONSIN
(1905-1936)

Introduction

Wisconsin is 56,066 square miles of rich glacier soil, stretched across the north central portion of the United States and defined by a ragged boundary. Lake Michigan marks the eastern border; the Mississippi River is the western boundary, Lake Superior and the Menominee, Brule, and Montreal Rivers the north. Only the southern border and some few miles at the state's northern limits follow a line not determined by natural waters. Some four thousand mapped lakes grace Wisconsin's interior.

The state's topography is varied, a composite of large areas of plains, smaller areas of stream-cut plateaus, large areas of erosion-worn bluffs. Three quarter of a million acres of swampland dot the central plain.[1] Cat Tail Valley is nestled in that plain.

The blond-haired French Jesuit explorer, Jacques Marquette, with his friend Louis Joliet had been there in the mid-seventeenth century. As they proceeded west from Green Bay along the Fox and Wisconsin Rivers, they carved Catholicism in the woods; the woodspeople made it prosper.

A century later they were followed by trappers who set their snares in the web of waterways, and then patiently waited for the fox, muskrat, marten and otter, who rarely failed them. And there were beaver, too, beautiful and prized. Native people were often their partners in this prosperous enterprise, among them the Winnebago, the Dakota, the Sioux and the Sac.

Trappers were soon followed by settlers and farmers who saw promise and fortune in the soil of Wisconsin. They created farms, built homes and established villages. In their persons they carried the civilization of their varied cultures and wedded it to the unspoiled land. The succession of people and professions was not without pain, however. Native

Americans with their wisdom and their particular ways were squeezed out of the new creation, a loss to the native people and the settlers alike.

Practiced in the ways of survival, the men and women who settled Wisconsin were skillful and confident. They believed they had the right to speak and to comment on a wide range of topics. One early country newspaper captured the prevalent spirit with these words: "This country should not only make its own hobnails but its own poetry. Truly the light is sweet."[2] Jessica Powers was steeped in that sweet light, and she indeed made her own poetry.

1

Summer in the "Cricket"

Some say the Wisconsin Dells and Lake Delton in Central Wisconsin had a mystic quality a half century ago. That was before amusement parks, trailer courts, pizza parlors, and high density zoning changed that particular river lake area, "the Dells," from a wooded retreat to a crowded resort, the way urbanization has affected most communities in America during the past fifty years.

But in the summer of 1936 Lake Delton was uncluttered. The little vacation cottages were unobtrusive, allowing the natural beauty of the woods and the still lake water to soothe rather than to stimulate. With the Great Depression then at its height in the United States people needed soothing.

That summer three women from the nearby farming community of Mauston, Wisconsin came to one of these cottages, named the "Cricket," eager for a week of nature, reading, laughter and companionship. Mary Walsh in her mid-thirties taught kindergarten in Mauston; before her lay forty-four years of teaching kindergarten to generations of Mauston families. Her own family lived on a farm in the outlying countryside, the area known as Cat Tail Valley.

Alice Keegan, Mary's aunt, a woman in her fifties, but considered "forever young" whom everyone called Allie, was an elementary school teacher in Milwaukee. She still considered Mauston her real home; always had, always would.

And there was Jessica Powers, thirty-one years of age, who might have been described as a farm woman, since the last eleven years had been spent keeping house for her two farmer brothers in Cat Tail Valley, faithful to an unspoken familial duty, after the death of their mother. She might have been described that way, but it would have been wrong. Those closest to her, including her companions at the "Cricket," knew she was more interested in cultivating words than in tilling the land. Jessica Powers was a poet.

Not everyone who writes verse is a poet. To be a kind of lightening rod for pure experience, to be alert and awake to the constant flow of experience, to live meditatively is to be a poet. To give form and voice to that experience is to write poetry. May Sarton, a twentieth-century American poet, describes the writing of poetry as "first of all a way of life, a discipline maintained in order to perfect the instrument of experiencing—the poet himself—so that he may learn to keep himself open and transparent, so that he may meet everything that comes his way with an innocent eye."[1] Jessica Powers encountered the world with an innocent eye.

Small both in stature and frame, her black hair styled in the bob of the thirties with flapper bangs and soft curls, she had a facial structure for which film makers search. Clean lines and well defined. When she occasionally wore long, dangling earrings and knickers she could look almost fashionable. Intelligent and witty, she loved laughter and music and children and books. And what else? In a little rhyme called "View of My Heart," handwritten in one of the notebooks of poems and verses she kept at that time, she muses about her loves, current and discarded.

> What do I love? Breakfast and luncheon and dinner
> And a warm white bed,
> The pine I planted out in the yard last summer
> And the sky over my head,
> Music and poetry and the stars of evening.
> What have I stopped loving? Shoes that are new
> And letter writing and mushrooms fried in butter
> And striped dresses and circuses and you.[2]

Her deepest love was still hidden, perhaps even from herself.

On the surface, Jessica Powers might have made a fine farm wife, but clearly her gaze and her heart were elsewhere, as noted in the verses above. One of the first things that people noticed about Jessica was her eyes. She seemed to look beyond you or through you. Not that she wasn't interested in you. Quite the contrary. Her brown eyes concentrated on you, brought you into the foreground, seeking to know you in some essential way. You sensed that she saw you through and through, but that was all right. She looked at everything this way. Birds, sky, trees, the inner world of pain and ecstasy. She fit Allen Ginsberg's description of the poet as one who probes into one subject or another, and ultimately probes into human consciousness.[3]

Catholic thought and religious practice, which at its best respects and supports both the intellectual and mystical life, framed and informed her constant artistic quest. By 1936 a large number of Jessica Powers's poems had been published, some in secular newspapers like the *Chicago Tribune* and the *Milwaukee Sentinel*, some in *The Forge*, the literary journal of the University of Chicago; some in religious journals and magazines like *Commonweal* and a few in the prestigious journal, *Poetry*. One of the *Poetry* selections, "Celestial Bird," later included in a book, *Poetry Out of Wisconsin* edited by the highly respected Wisconsin writer August Derleth along with eight others of Jessica's poems, is an excellent example of the probe into a particular subject that eventually uncovers another state of consciousness.

O sweet and luminous Bird,
having once renounced Your call, lovely and shy
I shall be hungry for the finished word.
Across the windy sky

of all voiced longing and all music heard.
I spread my net for Your bewildering wings,
but wings are wiser than the swiftest hands.
Where a bird sings

I held my heart, in fear that it would break.
I called You through the grief of whip-poor-wills,
I watched You on the avenues that make
a radiant city on the western hills.

Yet since I knew You not, I sought in vain.
I called You Beauty for its fleet white sound.

But now in my illumined heart
I can release the hound

of love upon whose bruising leash I strain.
Oh, he will grasp You where You skim the sod,
nor would Your breast, for love is soft as death,
swifter than beauty is, and strong as God. (31)

She was twenty-three when "Celestial Bird" was published.

When Mary and Alice, the teachers, and Jessica, the poet, came to the Cricket in the summer of 1936, they came with armfuls of books, most of them poetry. After breakfast they would push the dishes to one side of the table, open their books, and be lost until lunch. Sometimes they added the luncheon dishes to the breakfast collection as they read and read. Late one afternoon Mary's brother Bill, then in his late twenties, came to the Cricket with Tom Shelton, Frank Curran and Preston McEvoy, farmer friends from the Mauston area. As the moon appeared in the evening sky, someone suggested a walk to a nearby dam to see what the falls were like washed in moonlight. No one wanted to set aside the magic of the sight. Everyone's spirit seemed to be brightened, so much so, that when they returned to the cottage, the men stayed for a while, and the night was filled with conversation and laughter. The next morning Jessica felt the need to go over to the neighboring cottage to apologize in case their fun had disturbed anyone.

There were reasons beyond moonlight for Jessica's high spirits that July week. Her brother John had just been married to Catherine Pollard on July 11, 1936. Her younger brother Daniel had married the previous October, a double wedding, which joined Dan and Margaret Riddlestein and Tom Donovan and Marie Riddlestein. Jessica recorded the celebration in a humorous rhyme, describing herself, in her role of bridesmaid, as wearing a "dress of brownish wine/ And looking as if she needed a stein." Dan and Margaret had settled into one of the two farms owned by the Powers family. Now with John's marriage, the other farm would be cared for. Jessica was poised for a new life, her own life.

From the Cricket she wrote to a friend, Christopher Powell whom she had met during a brief period in Chicago when she worked as a secretary between 1923 and 1925. They had been corresponding with each other for seven or eight years, first while Christopher was a Dominican seminarian, and then after he left the Dominicans in 1930. They had been brought together by their common love of literature.

Jessica's letters to Christopher were ones of encouragement; he suffered from health problems, bouts of depression and a spiritual darkness: "I shall not attempt to tell you that the world is gay and colorful and pleasant, for I know you would not believe it," she wrote. "I should try to call you out of your mood. I might at least bring to your attention the splendor of the night—the stars of hope." Her letters were full of poetry, too, her own and others. (Elinor Wylie's "Velvet Shoes" was a favorite.) She inquired about Christopher's poetic efforts; she shared news.

The news from the Cricket proved to be a trajectory in the life of Jessica Powers. She wrote, "I am still in Mauston, but shall not be for long. The other of my two brothers was married in July—the 11th to be exact—and I am free to fly away. I should like to go to New York, but shall probably find myself settling in Chicago instead. Still, Chicago is beautiful to me; I always liked it tremendously well . . . It must be quite heavenly to roam the world, all its distant corners."[4]

New York was a dream. For years she had wanted to go there, believing that in New York she could learn more about the craft of poetry. The city's literary reputation weighed in against the reasons why she should stay in Wisconsin, or at the very least, Chicago. Jessica Powers had no financial resources. None. New York was expensive, and the Depression made living there even more difficult. Furthermore, her health was uncertain. While in Chicago in 1924 she showed some symptoms of tuberculosis, a disease which had caused her sister Dorothy's death in 1916. The threat of the tiny bacillus still haunted her. Although she had worked as a typist in Chicago, part of a secretarial pool, she had few business skills. Used to living in a close-knit, caring farm community where people looked out for one another, where religious and social values were shared, where there was both space and intimacy with nature, how would she manage in the accelerated, noisy, often impersonal, sometimes brutal atmosphere of New York? If others wondered, she did not.

Doubt and hesitation were relativized by the power of her purpose and a natural bent toward adventure. Because of her need for what she called "a fierce aloneness," a quality of being that is recognized as essential for the poet, people often mistakenly judged her to be shy or timid. The opposite was true. An unusual capacity for risk-taking, coupled with an exploratory nature propelled her into the New York pilgrimage. She was not fleeing from farm life and its demands so much as she was moving toward a new unknown horizon, one that could be approached only with trust and true feeling. She poured some of that longing for the unknown into an early poem, "Had I Lived Long Ago."

> "I would have wed a pirate chief,
> had I lived long and long ago,
> and made my home a ship that rides
> wherever winds can blow.
>
> I would have made me daring songs
> to fling against the sweeping gale—
> gay songs of strange and plundered shores,
> with notes like silver hail.
>
> But years have made their jest of me.
> Now I can only walk and sing
> a song about a broken heart. . .
> or any foolish thing."[5]

As the three friends piled their books and clothes into the car, and made ready to return to Mauston, neither Allie nor Mary knew that Jessica was resolved to go east. She was being called; it was that strong. And if she wanted for robust health, or money or a job, it didn't matter. She wanted more what New York had to offer.

But first she had to say good-bye to Cat Tail Valley, the open land where she first learned to see through to the heart of things, where she first heard inner music, winter music.

2

Cat Tail Valley: The Place and the Pioneers

Cat Tail Valley cannot be found on a map. Generally speaking, even the citizens of Wisconsin have never heard of it, probably because there are no physical boundaries. Yet fifty years ago, everyone knew where Cat Tail Valley was: twenty-one square miles that began several miles from St. Patrick's Catholic Church in Mauston, Wisconsin.

At the intersection of Highways O and K imagine a wheel fanning out two or three miles in all directions and you will have covered Cat Tail Valley. Its name was derived, so it is assumed, from the sweeps of cattails that accompany the stream that cuts through the valley.

In the early years of the twentieth-century, Cat Tail Valley contained about fifty-seven farms worked by the farmers and their families, and although they were usually no bigger than forty acres, a family could make a living from them. Maybe not a free-from-care living, but life could be sustained. These were the families of pioneers.

Before the pioneers, before 1843, Cat Tail Valley was populated mostly by Native Americans. But the potato famine in Ireland in the 1840s changed that as many Irish came to settle in the area. Jessica Powers's grandparents, maternal and paternal, were among the first.

Paternal Ancestry

John Powers and Catherine Hyde Powers were married in County Waterford, Ireland in 1842 and set sail for America four years later. They settled for a brief period at Indian Orchard, Massachusetts, but in 1850, they moved west, arriving finally in the town of Lemonweir in Juneau County, Wisconsin, two years after Wisconsin was granted statehood. With them was their first born child, Margaret, born in 1846, the year they left Ireland for the New World.

The newly arrived Powerses built a homestead near Seven Mile Creek, a tributary of the Lemonweir River, "the river of memory" in what is now referred to as Sevenmile Creek Township. With the raising of their log cabin the Powerses became one of the first pioneers in the region.

The area was (and still is) rich in timber: elm, maple, birch, evergreen and oak, and John Powers made his living principally as a lumberman, floating logs down the Wisconsin into which flowed the Lemonweir.

In 1852, the pioneer Powers family moved to a farm owned by Catherine's father, Patrick, who had preceded his daughter to America and who for a time worked in the sawmills at Mauston, Wisconsin. "The Hyde Farm" as it was generally known, was home to John Powers until his death. It was located across the road from the one room schoolhouse which the settlers of Cat Tail Valley built in the shade of a huge oak tree, which gave the school its early name, Burr Oak School. The Powers children could simply walk across the road to school, a convenience especially appreciated in the depths of Wisconsin winters.

John and Catherine Powers had other family nearby. Catherine's brother Thomas had settled in the Mauston vicinity, and was at one time sheriff of Juneau County. And there was John's half-brother Michael who had come to the Mauston region with his mother (John's step mother), Mary Slattery Powers. Known as Nan, she lived for an entire century, an energetic, intelligent woman who was proficient in nursing and who generously used her skills in the service of the Cat Tail Valley community. The Powers family was well represented in the valley.

More Irish soon arrived. There were Murphys, Walshes and O'Keefes, Keegans and Boyles, Dohertys, McGartys, Morrisseys, Pollards and more. It is not surprising, then, that when the Catholic parish was established in 1857 it was named for the patron saint of Ireland, Patrick. The church's steeple was and is the most prominent structure in the Mauston area, and from the open fields and farmlands of Cat Tail Valley it is easily visible, a reminder of the fundamental principle in the lives of the Irish men and Irish women who cultivated the land and built homes there.

John and Catherine (who became known as "Aunty John" in the tradition of Irish nicknaming) had nine more children after Margaret, four girls and five boys, all citizens of the new state of Wisconsin. Jessica's father, John, was the ninth, born in April of 1864, a year before the assassination of Abraham Lincoln.

John Powers, while "not tall," is remembered as very powerful and strong. His light auburn hair never turned gray, and he remained youthful and vigorous until his accidental death at age seventy-seven. And a strange accident it was. While climbing over a rail fence on his farm, the rail broke beneath him, and a large splinter pierced his body. The complications from this wound (possibly tetanus and blood poisoning) eventually brought about his death. His wife Catherine said that truthfully he was even older, probably closer to eighty, and if he had checked the fence more closely he could have gone on and on.

Catherine carried to America legends and songs of her beloved County Waterford. Her songs were in Gaelic as well as in English, and while she never claimed to have actually seen a leprechaun she did claim to have felt the effects of their antics, a snatched shawl lost on a country road, for example.[1] Jessica's childhood imagination was tuned to her grandmother's tales and her different language, remembered later in several poems: "I ask and ask, but no one ever tells me/what place we go when I meet Gaelic music." ("Gaelic Music," 77)

Around 1870 a second farm was purchased. It belonged to John's step brother, Michael, who had acquired it with his marriage to Catherine O'Keefe. And, of course, it was forever called the O'Keefe farm.

Although his parents were true pioneers, young John Powers's childhood was not marked by the problems typically associated with pioneer life. By the time of his birth the valley was pretty well settled. The farmers had built houses, barns, granaries, hen houses and sheds, and they were fairly self sufficient. They had their own milk, butter and eggs, and they made their own clothes. A typical farm had three to six cows, enough to provide dairy products for a family. The rich timber in the area provided additional livelihood for many, as it did for John Powers Sr. Sawmills were a familiar part of the Mauston landscape.

The residents of Cat Tail Valley seemed to be natural organizers. Burr Oak School was organized and built in 1863. There was a decision to divide the school year into two terms, a summer term and a winter term. Because the boys' labor was needed during the summer, they were limited to the winter term attendance. With the educational plan in place, Cat Tail Valley turned its attention to fire protection, a service badly needed and dearly wanted, yet not available. The farmers realized that numbers were important if they were to form their own fire insurance company, their ultimate goal. So they set out to talk to their neighbors in townships beyond Lemonweir. In between milking and planting they went to Lindina, to Summit and to Seven Mile Creek, bringing their message of strength in solidarity. In 1877 the Lindina Town Insurance Company, a citizens cooperative, was born. It continues to thrive generations later, a tribute to the farmers' intelligent perseverance.[2]

Hard work, social interdependence, strong religious identity, political acumen, pioneer daring—all these qualities enabled the people of Cat Tail Valley to shape a new life, one filled with promise for themselves and for their children. One factor was beyond their planning skills, however: disease. First, families lost their children to diphtheria which raged in the valley in the late 1870s. One family lost two young sons—aged seven and nine—on the same day. Even the legendary nursing skill of their grandmother Nan Slattery Powers could not help.

Diphtheria was followed by tuberculosis which killed children and adults alike, and again the disease swept through whole families. One can read the text of this sad chapter in St. Patrick's cemetery, at the edge of Cat Tail Valley.

Maternal Ancestry

The Irish also came to Lyndon Station, a close neighbor of Lemonweir and Cat Tail Valley. Among the first settlers was the Havey family who had endured a long and difficult nine-week sea journey from County Kildare. Without pausing for breath or rest they set forth immediately for the West. In Racine, Wisconsin, they stopped long enough to consult with another Irish family, the Keenas, who counseled the new immigrants to press on across Wisconsin and to locate Pat Hickey, a land agent who could advise them about their future. Hickey said the land all about—what is today Juneau County—was ideal for homesteading. Following an Indian trail, as Hickey told them to do, the Haveys came to the place that was to be a temporary home. In March of 1849 they built a log hut, stayed there until fall, and then moved to a site closer to water.

Other settlers joined the Haveys that year, among them the Keenas who in time would become the great grandparents of Jessica Powers, the same Keenas who had pointed the Haveys and others toward Juneau County. These early homesteaders called their town Kildare in remembrance of the place of their origins in Ireland.

By 1854 a first depot was in evidence. Other signs of village life soon followed: a post office, stores, town homes. And then the Milwaukee Railroad came to Kildare, enormously enhancing the town's corporate image. The growing sentiment was to recognize this new, vital presence. Kildare was not just a village, they said; it was a station, and the place name should reflect that, they argued. Furthermore, there was a bit of Irish competition at play. Not all the Irish settlers claimed Kildare as their birthplace. Some were from County Limrick, and they proposed that the village name be changed to Limrick Station. This was an unwinnable debate that finally yielded to compromise, and the village was eventually renamed Lyndon Station.

Among the pioneers *not* from Kildare was a young Scotsman, James Trainer, who with his brother Daniel arrived in 1850 when the village naming began. The Trainer brothers were from the Village of Dee near Castle Douglas in the Scottish lowlands. They set sail for America with very few provisions. They had their wit, their stamina, their ingenuity and their first edition of the poems of Robert Burns, revered Scottish poet, and a distant cousin of the Trainers. James and Daniel quickly entered the bustling life of Lyndon

Station, becoming expert woodsmen in every way. Before long the Trainers were the principal suppliers of logs to the mills at nearby Mauston. They were especially adept in the construction of corduroys and plank roads which enabled them to deliver logs the year round over roads that were frequently impassable.

One day James built a road to another pioneer cabin, one that belonged to the Keena family. Clearly it was one of the more important roads in James's life, for about a year later (1852) James married one of the Keena daughters, Catherine. James converted to Catholicism, and the couple settled into creative, frontier life. They worked at farming and their lumber business. Eight children were born to the Scotch-Irish couple. Delia, Jessica's mother, was the fifth child, born in 1867, two years after the end of the Civil War.

The agony of the Civil War affected Wisconsin as it did every state of the Union. Families yielded their sons and brothers, husbands and fathers to armies of the Union and to those of the Confederacy. There was sorrow on both sides. Endless sorrow. James Trainer, who resembled Abraham Lincoln with his dark eyes and narrow bearded face, joined the Lemonweir Minute Men. He was thirty-eight years of age then, and left behind his wife who was pregnant with their fourth child. It is very likely that he was part of Sherman's army. A letter to Catherine written March 14, 1865, from Fayetteville, North Carolina, acknowledges his gratitude for God's blessings even as it graphically describes the horrors of war:

> We have had a long hard march and don't know when or where it will end. The "Rebs" are right ahead of us. We were out skirmishing with them yesterday and the night before, and then out picketing all night where part of our brigade fought. Some dead. Rebs laying on each side of us. In the morning some of the company buried them. I was looking on."[3]

The letter recounts a number of other dangerous encounters, and even at that much is left unsaid. "I gave only a small account of the things I have witnessed. I have seen more than I wish to see again." James longed for his family. "It seems as though I would give anything to see you once more," he writes Catherine. And he urges her to "fix things to your wishes," and to get posts for the pastures so the colts will be cared for. He wants to know how the lumber business is. He hopes to be home for the next harvest. What he doesn't mention is his role in alleviating the army's most troublesome problem in North Carolina. Others, however, told the story.

The encamped army was rendered immobile because the Carolina spring rains had created rivers of mud, and the roads were impassable. James Trainer looked at the problem through his woodsman expertise and suggested that he and his fellow Wisconsinites build corduroy roads, as he had done in Lyndon Station. Soon other men joined the Wisconsin woodsmen-soldiers, and the road builders became known as the pioneer corps. These units were subsequently cited for their inventiveness and bravery which allowed the army to move on. Soon James Trainer moved even farther on, back to Lyndon Station, eager to be with Catherine and their four daughters. The newest baby, Margaret Agnes, later known in the family as Aggie, was born in 1865. Two years later Delia was born, followed by three boys. Quiet, capable, inventive James Trainer died in 1888 at age sixty-two. Like John Powers, his death was caused by an accidental fall, in his case a fall from a moving train. It was the same year that John Powers fell from his split-rail fence. Catherine survived James by twenty-two years, dying at age seventy-five.

British theologian A. M. Allchin observes that we have nothing which has not first been given to us. In particular, Allchin understands the givers to be one's parents and grandparents, the genetic reality which fashions all of us.[4] For Jessica Powers the gift was drawn from the well of Irish language, the spoken music that John M. Synge wrote into his plays. The sorrow of Ireland was there, too, along with a deep fidelity to the Catholic faith. And the gift was drawn from Robert Burns's lyrics, a branch of the family tree tended with respect. The volume of Burns's poems, carried from Scotland to America by James Trainer one hundred and fifty years ago, is now kept in the Mother of God carmel in Pewaukee, Wisconsin.

Jessica Powers's legacy from her grandparents, John and Catherine Hyde Powers and James and Catherine

Keena Trainer was above all a spirit of daring and risk, a spirit of determination, the spirit of a pioneer. No matter that she really knew only Catherine Hyde, "Aunty John." (Both grandfathers died before her birth, and she was five when Catherine Keena Trainer died.) She knew them all in her innermost being. Their lives nourished hers. Her inheritance included being born and reared in Cat Tail Valley, the place her people settled. They willed her the open spaces, the close-knit farming community, the majestic bluffs that keep watch over the farmlands, the whippoorwills and killdeers that echo through the valley.

Jessica Powers was born to pioneer, and the valley of her childhood helped forge that purpose. In truth she never underestimated the power of Cat Tail Valley in her life. Her poems about the valley were typically personified. In 1939 she published "The Valley of the Cat-Tails."

> My valley is a woman unconsoled.
> Her bluffs are amethyst, the tinge of grief;
> her tamarack swamps are sad.
> There is no dark tale that she was not told;
> there is no sorrow that she has not had.
> She has no mood of mirth, however brief.
>
> Too long I praised her dolors in the woods
> of the dark pines, her trees,
> and of the whip-poor-wills, her sacred birds.
> Her tragedy is more intense than these.
>
> The reeds that lift from every marsh and pond,
> more plainly speak her spirit's poverty.
> Here should the waters dance, or flowers be.
>
> Her reeds are proper symbols of a mother
> who from the primer of her own dark fears,
> as if the caroling earth possesses no other,
> teaches her young the alphabet of tears. (161)

In the valley of the cattails Jessica Powers first tasted loneliness. There she first learned the severe lessons of death.

3

Life—and Death—on the Farms

Very likely the Trainers of Lyndon Station and the Powers of Cat Tail Valley knew each other. In many ways they shared a common heritage. Both families were among the first settlers of Juneau County. Both came from Celtic stock. Both were in the lumbering business. And Catholicism was a central point of reference in both families.

So when John Powers II and Delia Veronica Trainer married in 1897—he was thirty-three and she was thirty—it must have seemed a natural alliance. Both their fathers had been dead for eleven years. Their mothers ably conducted the family businesses. And most importantly, two Powers farms became available to them. These farms were in close proximity to one another, country walking distance, on what is now Highway K. Aunty John Powers had already moved to town—to Mauston. There were no impediments, religious or practical, to marriage.

One farm, known as the Hyde Farm, was located across from the Burr Oak School. That was where John was reared and where his mother, Aunty John, had lived until recently. The other farm, the O'Keefe farm, was down the road from the first, a half a mile or so. John Powers I purchased it, though he never lived there. It was to this home that John brought his bride Delia. What Delia saw was a small, low-slung, unpainted building, with a partial second floor with two bedrooms. It was stark, yet beautiful in its own way. The weather-beaten house, edged with fragrant pines, was often flecked with sunlight. A woodburning stove that warmed the small house was also used for cooking. Kerosene lamps provided light. Water had to be pumped.

The land about was a gift of rich earth, perfect for dairy cows as well as for oats and corn and grains of all kinds. Delia immediately planted her own vegetable garden, and alongside the cows, she kept some lambs, who every once in a while, wandered into the kitchen-sitting room. Once John brought inside, for temporary shelter and nurturing, a black lamb that had been rejected by its mother.

Four children were born to Delia and John in this house between 1899 and 1906. Catherine Dorothy, called Dorothy was the eldest. John III, (Johnny), was born in 1901, followed by Agnes Jessica in 1905. James Daniel, (Dannie), was the last, born in 1906. Catherine and Daniel were not the only Powers children to be known by their middle names. At an early age, Agnes Jessica reversed the order of her given names. At her own initiative she became Jessica Agnes Powers; to the public, simply Jessica Powers.

She was born on February 7, 1905, in the middle of a fierce Wisconsin winter. The cold, the windswept farmhouse, the normal stresses of childbirth—all these challenged her to live. Some unconscious memory of the challenge seems to have stayed with her. Years later she wrote:

> I am a February child. I love these things—
> This broken shell of a house and the terrible song it sings.
> And winter shrieking wildly at this door.
> It has been here for eighty years or more.
> ("The House of the Silver Spirit," 125)

Winter appears over and over again as one of her most arresting poetic images. And with reason.

In the early years of this century, before central heating and indoor plumbing, before modernized farming methods, winter demanded preparation for its arrival and courage for its duration. John Powers often came into the kitchen shivering from the cold, after feeding the animals before the sun rose. His children, readying themselves for their daily walk to Burr Oak School sometimes helped to warm his feet. Jessica often undid her father's boots and rubbed his chilled feet with her hands that had been warmed at the wood stove minutes before. It was one of the rare moments of warmth in the old house. People remember the floors being so cold that when they visited to play cards they left on their overshoes.

The old farmhouse let in the sounds of winter, wolves howling in the distant tamarack, and whip-poor-wills lamenting. Once the wolves came right up to the house. They came not to harm, said Jessica's grandmother, but only out of hunger. Grandmother Aunty John Powers fed them and they left. This was simply the way winter was.

Burr Oak School held all eight grades in the space of one room, a common arrangement in rural areas of that period. Winifred Mullowney Powers was the school mistress who presided with wit and patience. Then as now the one room school provided an excellent education. Younger children were continually exposed to the higher levels of learning; so, rather than confining the student as the limited space might suggest, the student's intellectual environment was expanded and enriched. The school also served another purpose. Along with St. Patrick's church it helped knit together the rural community of Cat Tail Valley.

Other factors also bound the people together: family and farming needs of the community, and a fair amount of common ancestry. One's cousin was probably on a neighboring farm.

Not only did the Powers children go to school, on most days their dog did too. Delia would come looking for him carrying a stick to urge him back to the farm, much the way shepherds gather their straying sheep. The dog usually turned up at recess time, ready to play with children of all ages, and they were ready to play with him. He lived a goodly number of years for a dog, slowly wearing out. The infirmities and indignities of old age hit him hard, and when he was no longer able to walk, Dan Powers, the youngest of the Powers children, was assigned the sorrowful but necessary task of ending his days. Jessica retold the event in a poem, as she did so many experiences of her beloved Cat Tail Valley, later published in *The New York Times*, February 18, 1938:

Old Dog (Chuck)

Lifting my gun to end his agony
I saw my old dog's eyes
He turned his head; they beamed with pity,
Then darkened with a terrified surprise.
He knew the meaning of a pointed gun
Yet he did not attempt to rise and flee
Nor whimper even once; the thing was done
A stricken look was all he gave to me.

My friends say I go cautiously of late
Subdue my speech and curb a wily pen
I think of the devotion in those great
Dark eyes with knowledge of betrayal there
And I walk gently with my fellow men
It would be too much in one life to bear
That wounded look again.

For an imaginative, deeply intuitive and sensitive child like Jessica, the short walk home from school had its share of terror. There was, for instance, the old bridge that created a safe passage across a stream. But to young Jessica the dark secrets underneath the bridge were reason enough to race home. Once her mother walked her back to the bridge (she must have been eight or nine) and looked under it with her to convince Jessica that no ogres were in residence there. Again, the experience was transformed into verse.

Here is the bridge of my childhood marked with fear.
I thought an ogre waited under it,
quick to devour if I should venture near.
I ran at sight of it. My sandals hit

the brown dust of the roadway going by.
Oh, it was like a day of lifted dread
when I grew bold enough to peer and pry,
seeking the monster, finding peace instead.

Fled is that childish fear. My thoughts are couched
in grown-up wisdom now, and yet I find
that worse than ogres are the dark shapes crouched,

lurking beneath the bridges of my mind.
("Old Bridge," 104)

There were more family than ogres, however, in the valley.

Indeed, at times it must have seemed as if the world were peopled with cousins. Farm families tended to be large, and at celebrations of one kind or another, a number of children of all ages were likely to be related to one another. This web of relationships had its stresses as well as its securities. On one occasion, at a farm social, some of the older girls came upon Jessica talking to her dolls. They couldn't resist making fun of her and she couldn't resist crying. Among the older girls was a cousin who stayed to comfort the distraught child, a kindness that was never forgotten. When she was in her eighties Jessica sent a religious card to that same Good Samaritan cousin with the memory of the long ago good deed.[1]

Growing up on the farms of Cat Tail Valley was good. Nature has her own liturgical moments: the passing of seasons, the glad reception of sun and rain, even the snows of winter. The farm people highlighted these natural rhythms by connecting them, perhaps unconsciously, to the Church's liturgical calendar. On St. Patrick's Day the farmers planted their potatoes. In mid-summer, on August 15th, the feast of Mary's Assumption, friends and families from the towns joined the valley farmers for the threshing of the grains. In the midst of work, a festive feeling prevailed. The women cooked, children participated both in the fields and in the indoor work of preparing and serving food, and community bonds strengthened as men, women and children worked and celebrated together.[2]

Then there were the intentional, explicit Catholic rituals, ancient and reliable, sustenance for the pioneers and their families. Horse and wagons regularly took the Valley people to St. Patrick's church on Sunday mornings, a distance of five miles from the Powers's farms. At Christmas time the wagons were festooned with bells, and families, bundled tightly against the cold and the wind, their breath like low flying clouds before them, musically rode into Mauston for 5:00 a.m. Mass, the spire of St. Patrick's church (always visible in Cat Tail Valley) encouraging them forward.

St. Patrick's was not only the center of the Valley people's regular worship, it was the place where they marked the great transitions of life, baptisms, marriages, funerals. When she was eleven years old Jessica moved through the first of a series of funerals that profoundly affected her all the days of her life. Dorothy, the eldest of the Powers's children, beautiful, bright Dorothy died of tuberculosis. The year was 1916. Dorothy was almost seventeen.

Tuberculosis raged through families and communities in the nineteenth and first half of the twentieth centuries in most of the known world. Sanitariums dedicated to the treatment of the dread disease dotted the landscapes of many countries, telling a story of total vulnerability before the mystery of illness. Medical experts believed that high elevations with brisk and bracing mountain air could cure the disease. Sanitariums were designed with long, outdoor porches where patients rested and slept by day and sometimes by night. At Saranac Lake in upstate New York was probably the most famous curative colony in the United States. Its visibility came from the celebrities who went there for cures themselves, or to visit family or friends with tuberculosis. Only those with money could afford such private facilities. But most states also had sanitariums, called statesans. In adulthood, Jessica Powers would become well acquainted with the routines of the Wisconsin statesan at Stevens Point.

But in 1916, while thousands were dying on European battlefields during the First World War, thousands more were being felled by a tiny bacillus, microscopic in size, too clever for the medical wit of that period. The farm families of Cat Tail Valley were not spared the bacteria's devastation. One hoped to finesse a way through the destructiveness of the disease with fresh air, fresh food, rest and good luck. The finesse did not work for Dorothy Powers.

During the winter of 1916 the feared signs of the disease's presence first appeared. The cough. The loss of appetite. Fatigue, bone weary fatigue. The alabaster color. The weight loss. Still, the family hoped and prayed. In April and May and early June, Dorothy's condition was so severe that she was confined to the farmhouse, in the downstairs bedroom off the kitchen, John and Delia's room. Jessica's indoor chores—more of them now because her mother was occupied with Dorothy—kept her close by her sister. On June 8th Jessica was drying some cups in the kitchen when her mother told her the stunning news. Dorothy was dead. Many years later, after a lifetime of poetry, after decades of experience as a Carmelite nun, she wrote in her journal, "My life would have been much different if Dorothy had lived." What did she mean? Would her life choices have been different had Dorothy's life gone on? Perhaps. What seems clear is that Jessica was happy to have a beautiful, older sister to follow and learn from. The deepest learning, however, was her first lesson in bereavement. She learned how loss penetrates to the center of one's life, a chilling and complete experience. Death is death. It is forever. Her uncle Frank (Delia's brother) used to say whenever anyone died that he or she had solved the great mystery. (The trouble was that no one else could get in on the mystery.) Jessica kept the saying among her inner treasures, as she kept so much of the flow of experience, and over sixty-five years later released it in a poem.

> My uncle had one sober comment for
> all deaths. Well, he (or she)
> has, he would say, solved the great mystery.
> I tried as child to pierce the dark unknown,
> straining to reach the keyhole of that door,
> massive and grave, through which one slips alone.
>
> A little girl is mostly prophecy.
> And here, as there before,
> when fact arrests me at that solemn door,
> I reach and find the keyhole still too high,
> though now I can surmise that it will be
> light (and not darkness) that will meet the eye.
>
> ("The Great Mystery," 100)

St. Patrick's Church helped people deal with that soul-sore mystery. Dorothy's young friends and relatives gathered in the church to help ease her into another life and to help ease themselves into life without her. There were active and honorary pallbearers, according to gender. The active pallbearers were young men and boys. The honorary bearers were young women. One of them, her cousin Frances Powers, died of tuberculosis the following month.

The deep Celtic faith in the rightness of God's ways carried the Powers family through the dark loss of Dorothy. After Delia and John buried their child in the parish cemetery, they gathered their remaining three children and returned to their farm to do the work that was theirs. The cattle needed tending. (The medal of St. Brigid, patroness of cattle which had a prominent place in the barn was not sufficient. St. Brigid, good as she was, would not milk the cows.) Soon it would be the Fourth of July, and the potatoes planted on St. Patrick's Day must be dug. August and threshing time would soon arrive. In the face of loss the valley continued to plow and plant and reap. Nature not only chastises, she encourages.

Nature encouraged and sustained Jessica. That summer, the summer of Dorothy's leaving, Jessica found comfort in the alfalfa field, in full bloom. The evening time was the best. It was then that country fragrances were most comforting, she felt.[3]

John Powers's political responsibilities were waiting and that helped. He had been in public life for years, holding many different elected offices. Only recently he had been elected chairman of the town of Lemonweir. The Powers's kitchen was often the setting for political discussions, about state and national issues as well as local. Jessica liked to listen in on these conversations. They signaled a world beyond the farmlands, a world of ideas, of new things to be learned. A great deal of work lay ahead for John, and it was welcome. Work is one of the ancient healers; John Powers knew that.

But Delia's garden and the routines of farmwork were not sufficient balm for her. She grieved for Dorothy, and Jessica grieved for her mother.[4] In truth, Delia may have been anticipating the emptiness of life without both her daughters. Delia was well aware that Jessica, too, would soon leave the farm, at least for each school week. It was time for Jessica to attend the Catholic school—the Sisters School—in Mauston.

Attendance at the school was a requirement of St. Patrick's pastor, Father Schleicher for those children who would participate in the solemn ritual of receiving Holy Communion. At that time, the second decade of the twentieth century, solemn communion occurred around age thirteen.

It was customary for the children of Cat Tail Valley, who attended either the Sisters School or Mauston High School, to board in town. One Sunday morning in September of 1916 John and Delia and their three children climbed into their wagon for the five mile drive to Mauston, to Sunday Mass at St. Patrick's church. Clothes and food for the week were packed for Johnny, a student at Mauston High School, and for Jessica, who was to spend her first night away from home.

Jessica knew this trip to Mauston was different from others. She missed Dorothy. Already, she missed the pine trees and the whip-poor-wills. But she was also expectant. Mauston was a door way. She sensed that. What she did not know was that on the other side of the threshold she would meet a person who would forever influence the direction of her life.

4

Mauston, on the River of Memory

The people of Mauston say that the river which winds through the town, the Lemonweir River, means "the river of memory," a name drawn from the Sac language, but an appropriately romantic designation for the Irish who built the town. The story is that a General Maughs, who gained his rank in the Indian Wars, plotted the town in 1848 around the time that Jessica Powers's pioneer grandparents arrived in the area. The general apparently liked his title because he kept it as a civilian lumberman. The land around the Lemonweir was rich in lumber of all kinds, and the general immediately saw the possibilities. He not only established one of the first mills, he also named the town after himself. But first he dropped the "gh" from his name. Both he and the town were called Mauston.[1]

When Jessica Powers rode into Mauston in September of 1916 she rode through a recognized hub for Wisconsin's lumber industry. Several lumber yards, a general store, a town elementary school, St. Patrick's Catholic Church and school, a jail, Mauston High School, a few specialized shops, town homes—all these combined to give a productive, even prosperous look to the town.

In some of the homes children from the Cat Tail Valley farms lived during the school week. Dorothy had stayed at the Kate O'Brien home in town, and an O'Brien child had also been lost to tuberculosis. Some farmers felt there was a risk in town, but the Powers family seemed to realize that the disease was everywhere. And children had to go to school, they had to receive the sacraments, and they had to have some place to live.

The widow Minnie Saunders boarded a half dozen or so young students each term. It was here that the Powers family headed after Sunday Mass. Johnny Powers, age fifteen, knew the routine. Now he and his little sister, Jessica were settling in without Dorothy. They joined five other young people from the farms, all known to one another.

The Saunders home was an easy walk to the Sisters school for little Jessica, and experienced Johnny could manage the short journey to Mauston High School. Very likely Jessica called on her guardian angel for particular watchfulness, on this, her first night away from home in a strange house. Her guardian angel remained a very personal presence in her life always. Her favorite childhood prayer was to her angel.

> Holy Angel guard my slumbers
> through the danger of the night
> Hold your snowy wings around me
> Angel beautiful and bright.[2]

The routine was for the families to unpack the food (a bit of meat, cheese, bread, milk and oats) and to set it in the Widow Saunders's larder; to put the school clothes in the proper place; to say good-bye to their children; and to return to the farms and the work that could not be postponed. Not until Friday, at the end of the school week, would the children return to Cat Tail Valley. Meanwhile, Minnie Saunders's home was their home for five days of the week. Jessica was to spend six years with Minnie Saunders, seventh and eighth grades at the Sisters School, and four years at Mauston High School. These were years when she joined the other boarders in parties—they would roll up the rugs, turn on the gramophone, and dance away. During Lent the youngsters would say the rosary several evenings a week, Jessica often leading the young pray-ers through the mysteries of the New Testament.[3]

Whatever heaviness Jessica might have felt at leaving her mother and father for the world of town and religious schooling was lightened when she walked into St. Patrick's School. Sister Lucille Massart, O.P., who taught the seventh and eighth grades, entered Jessica's world, and introduced her to what May Sarton refers to as the holy game of poetry.[4] More importantly she invited Jessica to play the game with great seriousness and purpose.

Sister Lucille was small in stature and large in energy. Dressed in the white habit of the Dominican Order, she was like a protective yet daring angel, urging her young students to stretch their minds and spirits as far as they could, and then some. She loved language, knowing instinctively that language, particularly artful language—poetry—was to encounter otherness, certainly a goal of religious life. In the classroom and outside Sister Lucille peeled back the secrets of the world of words. The school playground was small and usually given over to the boys' intense baseball games (baseball was serious business in the Mauston-Cat Tail Valley environs), so Sister Lucille and her assortment of devotees, steered away from the playground and instead walked up and down the sidewalks, looking, listening, discovering the natural elements of poetry all around them. The walked during noontime in Mauston. Each day at twelve, like an angelus in motion, the procession passed the Mauston jail. The prisoners, lined up at the windows, waited, ready to greet Sister Lucille and her company with cheerful waves. On and on they walked in the great tradition of Aristotle's peripatetic teaching.

When Jessica Powers entered the wordworld of Sister Lucille, the nun knew a true although obviously untrained poet had joined the ranks of her seventh graders and noontime walkers. She saw a child able to look at the world as if it had just been created.[5] This order of looking is like unto prayer; "The answer to the prayer is the poem which describes the object and also does something more, is something more than the object itself."[6] Sister Lucille encouraged Jessica to respond, to write *her* poems. And she did. At age eleven, in the year 1916, the year the United States entered the First World War, Jessica Powers met her Muse. And she never forgot her. She poured out her feelings in a poem she called "To Sister Lucille."

> The little years that rose and came between us,
> That took you from me with a gesture gay,

Are baffled at my cool and wide-eyed laughter,
And wonder that I sing with you away.

They do not know that you are always with me;
I hear your voice in every song-bird call;
I know your whisper in the reeds of marshes,
Your laughter in a silver waterfall.

The sunbeams are your words: they say "I love you"
I drink your kiss from every gypsy breeze,
And little ribbon roads are singing of you
A little song of poignant memories.

The little years that rose and came between us
Have tried to still my love of you in vain;
For all the world conspires by wind and magic,
To keep you mine until you come again.[7]

Like many young poets, Jessica wished to write only of love.

Poetry began to fill the hollow in Jessica that Dorothy's death had carved. At Christmas the following year—she was twelve—she gave her family a handwritten book of original rhymes dedicated to her parents.[8] There is a poem "To Daddy" full of pious Christmas wishes, a poem of ardent love for her mother, again ending with heavenly blessings. Humorous poems are saved for her brothers. Johnny's verses are about his new pair of long pants and vest (he's at an age to care about such things), and Dannie's recounts his courage at the appearance of rats in the farmhouse. "When in the pantry off the room/ You heard a mouse's tap/ You didn't run to get a broom,/ But jumped in mamma's lap." Dorothy, dead a year and a half, also receives a poem. A lily, growing in flowery mead, is the subject of the meditation. Dorothy is another lily, "that budded by my side in ardent love." To Dorothy she pours out her "restless soul," a theme and description of her being to which she held on throughout her life and work.

Her final piece in the Christmas book of 1917 is about herself:

Her hair is very black
    She's as naughty as can be,
And that little girl alas!

Is no other girl than me.
Jessie.

Altogether not great poetry, perhaps not even poetry at all, still one sees in this early verse the choice made for gift to others, some crafting of feeling (romantic and religious), and a movement from the concrete and specific (love for mother or father, a lily in the mead field) to the more universal, in her case, the religious understanding of the restless soul. It is the embryo of what May Sarton describes as poetry, "The perpetual reincarnation of the spirit through a concrete image."[9]

St. Patrick's Church, then, as now, is distinguished by full-length stained glass renderings of certain saints. Paul and Joseph, Catherine (of Alexandria) and Agnes, Aloysius Gonzaga, John the Baptist and Peter, Rose of Lima. The Blessed Virgin Mary is depicted as a child, and again, carried into heaven ("assumed" is the term in Catholic teaching)—they line both sides of the nave. Jessica liked to go to Mass in their presence. She would pretend that the windows were really plain and that the saints came just to be at Mass. There they were, in all their glory, radiant with sunshine! Later she wrote about them.[10]

Through periods of redecoration the unusual stained glass windows have stayed, along with the statue of St. Patrick, given to the church by one of the pioneer Powers. Today the statue is not in the front of the church as it was in Jessica's childhood but discreetly in the rear, except for the days surrounding the feast of St. Patrick, on March 17th. Then the patron of Ireland is brought forward to reside, briefly, at an honored front position.

Life in Mauston was abundant for Jessica. There was the beginning of poetic structure for her imagination and for her deepening devotional life. There were times of fun, too. The future was full of expectancy and mystery. Political concerns sometimes brought her father into town (she loved to listen to the artful talk of politics), or service to the church (the men of St. Patrick's fetched coal and performed other needed chores), so Jessica's homesickness was muted. Sorrow seemed a little softer.

All that changed on a beautiful day in May, 1918. John Powers had brought a wagon load of coal to the church, unloaded it, and was about to drive home when he was overcome with dizziness and shortness of breath. Several people noticed his distress and rushed to his aid, but were unable to remedy the massive heart attack that claimed his life at age 53. Jessica was thirteen years of age, on the rim of womanhood, filled with unknown longings, painful in the way of youth. This new pain though was different, the loss of what had been, not the vague loss of what might be.

St. Patrick's Church was filled with those who wanted to pay their final respects to this son of the area's first pioneers. He was spoken of as "square in his dealings and the friend of all." His years of elected public service raised the level of public mourning. The saints looked upon all those gathered in remembrance and prayer; once again they arrived in time for Mass.

The death of John Powers meant serious changes for his family. Johnny's schooling ended, since he was needed on the farm. The other children continued their education. Jessica was about to enter Mauston High School and Dannie was in the Sisters School. Delia decided to move to the farm across from Burr Oak School. It was smaller and easier to manage. The farm that bore Jessica in "her frosty womb" ("The House of the Silver Spirit," 125) was rented out.

In the autumn Jessica returned to Minnie Saunders. There was a natural excitement associated with entering the larger world of Mauston High School, but it was dulled by the continuing assertiveness of death. Still, Jessica's enthusiasm carried her forward. There were new things to learn—Latin among them—and the school paper offered both motivation and possibilities for poetry. Jessica regularly saw Sister Lucille, who continued to discover in her young poet an uncanny eye and a natural music that could create lyrics out of the stuff of ordinary life. Sister Lucille knew this gift of language to be of God, and she did everything she could to nurture it whenever Jessica visited her. She gave her books of poetry so she would not be alone in the rarified realm of image and meaning. She encouraged Jessica to make the most of nature that served as her principal laboratory of experience. Sister Lucille ratified Jessica's instinctual knowledge that there was more to a flower or a bird or an emotion than at first appeared. And just as Sister Lucille opened up a world of feeling and form, she also opened a door to the experience of God. Jessica found that prayer occurred in places other than church. It happened in open fields, under the stars, in the stirrings of the secret heart. It may be that with her father's death coming so quickly after Dorothy's, her vocation, her call to become who she was in her inner self, took clearer form. Death, not lyrical flights, is the real intimate of poetry, writes Patricia Hampl.[11]

With death as a shadowy companion, the routines of Mauston and of Cat Tail Valley—including the sacraments of solemn communion and confirmation (she chose Lucille for her confirmation name)—grounded her. Still, the tugs and pulls of growing up were present. Even with close friends, a social life sprinkled with hints of possible romance, a clearly developing talent for writing, and always the deepening sense of God's majesty in the universe, Jessica moved through her teen years feeling unbeautiful.[12] Her perception of unattractiveness in her youth may have been an indirect means to develop sufficient ego strength to pursue a creative life rather than the conventional, socially normative one, typically laid out for women in the early years of this century.

Feminist scholar and fiction writer Carolyn Heilbrun posits an even bolder thesis, namely that:

> with highly gifted women, as with men, the failure to lead the conventional life, to find the conventional way early, may signify more than having been dealt a poor hand of cards. It may well be the forming of a life in the service of a talent felt, but unrecognized and unnamed. This condition is marked by a profound sense of vocation, with no idea what that vocation is, and by a strong sense of inadequacy and deprivation.[13]

The Heilbrun thesis seems to fit Jessica Powers in many respects although not all. Not only was Jessica aware of her own talent; others also recognized and named it. She did have a sense of vocation, searching for something different. It seemed to be writing. Or was it really a search for a way of life, a possibility not necessarily exclusive of the other. How does one pursue a way of life when the circumference of one's own life includes limited financial resources (two heavily mortgaged farms), family responsibilities, social and cultural expectations for young farm women? What does the president of the high school poetry society do after graduation? Go to teachers' college? Marry? Work on the family farm? Enter the convent? Jessica Powers did none of these. She and her family scraped together enough money to allow her, briefly, to enter the world of higher education—Jesuit education—at Marquette University in Milwaukee. The same wagon that expanded her circle of living from Cat Tail Valley to Mauston now took her to Milwaukee, a wider world still. It was September 1922. Jessica was seventeen. She brought with her a love for the land, the pain of death, a haunting loneliness and a deep desire for something more. She brought with her spiritual knowledge.

> One time as a child on the rim of creation
> I walked into the area left by the sun.
> The house that I lived in by distances dwindled,
> and the earth rolled away like a top that was spun.
>
> I climbed out of my body and wandered and wandered
> through the fabulous meadows that constitute sky.
> The clouds like some great colored snowdrifts were shoveled
> to the east of the path I was travelling by.
>
> The last thing I saw on the earth was a church spire
> in the city of Mauston below me and far.
> I stopped at the gate of the silver-blue seamen
> who teach the young west how to anchor a star.
>
> I came back from my journey so clean and so shining
> that no matter what dark fell I still would be free.
> I climbed into my body out back of the pine trees,
> and night drifted down over Mauston and me.
>
> ("One Time as a Child," 136)

This granddaughter of pioneers, already knowledgeable about interior paths, had come to a new frontier.

5

Big Cities: Milwaukee and Chicago

In the first quarter of the twentieth century, Mauston was a city of manageable proportions, with two thousand men, women and children. A person could feel at home there. Furthermore, branches of Jessica Powers's family were spread throughout the small lumber city; she was well sheltered in Mauston. But security was not enough. The searching, the longing—for knowledge and for beauty, she said—drew her out of Mauston, and into a larger world of learning, the world of the university. This academic universe also meant the rhythms of big city life. Specifically, Milwaukee.

Marquette University helped her enter into the bustling, brewery city.

Milwaukee, the largest city in Wisconsin (44.1 square miles), curves along a bay in Lake Michigan. Looking eastward, one sees waterways dotted with boats and ships, everything from freighters to sailboats. To the west are the highways winding past wooded farmlands and the great abundance of lakes that refresh generation after generation of Milwaukeeans. All this Jessica Powers looked out upon. And there was more. The city was—and is—laced with parks, canals and bridges, fit subjects for the painters of landscapes and cityscapes.

Milwaukee is a city that takes pride in certain values: good health, good education, safety, culture, sound economy, consistently good government. It has also been, from the beginning, a community of genuine cultural diversity. When Jessica arrived in Milwaukee in 1922, approximately nineteen percent of the population was foreign born, a large proportion of them German. Many of the original German immigrants who came in the mid-nineteenth century were, in fact, wealthy and cultured refugees fleeing from unsuccessful attempts to overthrow German monarchies. They put their talents and energies into the new homeland, founding theaters, music societies and intellectual associations of various kinds. During the first World War, however, anti-German feeling (which ran high throughout the country) resulted in a prejudice against this particular stream of culture in Milwaukee. German streets and German foods, for example, were renamed. German music was quieted.

Other nationalities were found in Milwaukee: Poles, Czechs, Italians and Irish. And somewhere between six and seven thousand African-Americans were living and working in Milwaukee in 1922. They came at the time of the First World War to fill labor shortages and then settled there, putting down roots, establishing businesses. Generally speaking, African Americans found a welcome in the city. After all, Milwaukeeans were early supporters of abolition and made their convictions known in different ways, from harboring escaped slaves to supporting abolitionist writing. Today the city strains under racial tensions (much like other urban centers), while still exhibiting a willingness to experiment in order to expand opportunity for African-Americans. In recent years, for example, several innovative schools for the education of African-American males have been established.

Missing in this rich mixture of peoples—at least in significant numbers—were the native Americans, those who had given Milwaukee its name. The Potawatomi, the Menominee, the Chippewa, like other Indian nations elsewhere in North America, were left with little choice but to cede their territories to the United States. Almost a hundred years before Jessica Powers took up her brief residence in Milwaukee the once mighty Potawatami People were moved by wagon train to Kansas.[1] Indians had been part of Jessica's own world, sprinkled in the population of Cat Tail Valley, (there was always an Indian baseball team, for example). They lived in the plains of her imagination:

When the dead white mists
creep up in the evening rain,
out of the half-blurred swamp
the ghostly cities rise:
wigwams like gulls' wings spread,
hundreds across a plain;
and I look out on them
through my mother's mother's eyes.[2]
("Wigwams," 168)

A familiar current of religious-cultural-social life was evident to Jessica in Milwaukee: Catholicism. Many of the Germans, Poles, Italians and Irish brought with them the practice of the Catholic faith. The first German bishop in the United States was Bishop John Martin Henni, who was also the first bishop of Milwaukee, appointed in 1840. Marquette University, a non-sectarian institution of higher education operated by the Society of Jesus (the Jesuits) was begun as a religious academy in 1857. As it developed into a university it retained much of the religious ethos of the Jesuits. Marquette was the reason Jessica left Mauston for Milwaukee at the age of seventeen.

The story of Marquette University is one of rapid evolution, from St. Aloysius Academy to St. Gall's Academy to Marquette College to the status of a university, fifty years later in 1907. As a university in the second decade of this century it housed a law school, a college of applied science and engineering, a college of economics, a conservatory of music, schools of medicine and dentistry in addition to a training school for nurses, a college of arts and sciences and the school of journalism. The expansion, including acquisition of property and new building, was possible because of the donated services of the highly trained Jesuits. The Marquette University Bulletin for 1922-1923 highlights the Jesuits' contributions in terms of public service. "For more than twenty-five years the faculty of Marquette have been devoting themselves in this manner to the people of Milwaukee, and they will continue to do so in the future." The bulletin goes on to say that money is needed in order to grow, but that raising tuition will not be an option; rather, public spirited citizens "must shoulder the responsibility for this resource that benefits the entire community."

In 1922, two years after a constitutional amendment granted women the right to vote, Marquette University, like many other private and public institutions in American society, maintained a male-only policy in its various schools. The college of arts and sciences, where Jessica might logically have gone to pursue her study of literature, was closed to her. The school of journalism, however, was open, a fact not lost on intelligent, enthusiastic women eager for higher education. Sixty-three percent of the 1922 first-year class was female. All of the faculty were male, mostly Jesuits. The school's acceptance of women was highlighted in the informational materials with such observations as, "Unlike most professions journalism does not look upon the woman who practices it as an exception." Readers were reminded that women writers, in poetry and fiction, were often situated in the field of journalism. The reminder read like a promise to Jessica Powers.

At Marquette, journalism and literature were partners. Again, the University Bulletin for that year reads: "It is not only in the daily papers that the journalist fulfills his vocation . . . in the history of English and American literature . . . newspaper work and reporting are the surest steps to literary success and fame." In all probability, Jessica would have chosen the Journalism School even if Arts and Sciences had accepted women. It was, in many ways, the perfect fit.

Marquette talked about journalism as a genuine vocation, one akin to medicine or teaching or law. How could one judge an authentic vocation? The first mark, they said, was a natural talent which included the desire to write, to peruse and to record one's experiences, observations and criticisms of the life going on all around one. A deep sympathy with everyday life, its pathos and humor, its hopes, fears, aspirations, impulses and motives is part of this first clue. Prospective students were told that the journalist is one who is always seeing in the ordinary affairs of daily life the revelation of the mind and soul of the human being. The school would build on these natural inclinations and leanings by providing a curriculum that included logic, metaphysics, philosophy and ethics as well as the practical skills of the newsroom. The School of Journalism offered Jessica all this and more. It offered courses in the English department. One course in particular must have been particularly attractive to her, a course simply called "Poetry." It included theories of English prosody, the part played by Latin Christian hymns in determining the metrical principles of modern languages, the romantic revival of Wordsworth and Coleridge, and Catholic poets like Patmore, Francis Thompson and others, as well as contemporary Catholic poets.[3]

Shortly after Jessica arrived on campus in September of 1922 the university paper, *The Marquette Tribune*, announced cash prizes for poetry, namely Christmas verses that could be used on postcards. That and the poetry columns in the Milwaukee newspapers—also poetry for pay—stimulated an already eager and highly motivated young woman from Mauston.

The *Milwaukee Sentinel* published a poetry column called "The Percolator." Jessica never failed to read it. In many ways it served a purpose similar to that of the Dublin Post Office in Ireland, a kind of bulletin board where young writers, full of courage and hope, could go public. "The Percolator" introduced Jessica Pegis, poet and short story writer and wife of philosopher Anton Pegis, to Jessica Powers, student and poet. At first the relationship flourished through paper and ink and shared insights. It would be years before they would meet in New York City.

Chicago newspapers were readily available too, sparking her interest in the city, where fog creeps in on little cat feet, as Carl Sandburg described it. Another enormous treasure was the library, and not just one library, but libraries. Both the university and the city housed all kinds of literature waiting to be read. For Jessica, library reading rooms were places of gracious hospitality. All of this intellectual stimulation was augmented by the opportunities for an intensified religious practice. The Jesuit church, the Gesu, was near at hand. Daily Mass was offered on campus. The sodality, closely associated with the Jesuits, focused on Christian character formation. The Marquette sodality had several sections, one of which was devoted to literature. Members could contribute articles, support Catholic publications and even sell them. In the area were also third orders, associations of lay people who follow similar rules of life as those in religious orders.

Jessica lived with a family distantly related to her, the Geraghtys. Sarah Geraghty taught school; her sister, Aunt Mame, kept house and cared for the maiden ladies' two nieces, Mae (age eight) and Peggy (age five). The aunts and the little girls shared a duplex apartment on Farwell Avenue in a house owned by the children's father, who was separated from his wife. He was, at the time, living on a farm near Franksville, south of Milwaukee. In many ways, this was the perfect arrangement for Jessica. She was beginning to show signs of ill health and Aunt Mame watched over her carefully. The Geraghty family children delighted her, as all children did. She felt secure enough to roam intellectually and aesthetically.

The Marquette University adventure ended quickly—the Powers family simply did not have enough money to finance more education—and Jessica returned to the farm, to Cat Tail Valley in the winter of 1923. She left several new friends and the leaving was full of heartbreak. She wrote to one, Aimee, a few lines of young love and longing.

> I used to be afraid to say "I love you"—.
> You seemed so cool and certain, so apart,
> From sentiment and love with its emotion,
> I tried to storm the walls about your heart.
> You baffled me . . . until that last great moment
> I came to say good-bye with many fears;
> And as I paused to leave you I was startled . . .
> Your eyes were filled with tears.[4]

After good-byes and tears, Jessica gathered her belongings, including the few books she had acquired, folded up her disappointment and went home. She was not morose—she had too much humor and laughter stored within for that—and she was not resigned. The longing to write was not packed away. Her return to Cat Tail Valley was a temporary detour. She wanted more. She knew she had to feed the lyricism lodged in her spirit; her songs demanded release.

> Born in the valley of the reeds
> I am no less a reed than they
> brown-cowled and without blossom to this day.

My heart upon dark water feeds
I stir to music from the hills
lament of evergreens and whippoorwills.

My songs are reeds; out of the damp
Doomed marshes and choked ponds they rise,
Each with an aspiration to the skies.

My songs are cat-tails in a swamp
Wisconsin born, each marked to be her daughter,
Those to the sky, those bent back to the water.[5]

At home in the valley she felt a oneness with the cattails, as emptiness and aspiration mixed.

Aunt Carrie was at the farm a good bit, helping out, and providing practical companionship for Delia, so Jessica was somewhat free to roam in search of the right setting to cultivate her poetry. She decided to try Chicago. She knew how to type. She was sure there would be work for her there. Fortunately, some family would be close by. Dene Harrington Fisher, a sister-in-law of Jessica's godmother, Nellie Harrington, owned an apartment house in Chicago. She had available a large one room furnished apartment. Best of all, libraries would be at hand, in addition to concerts and plays. Chicago was even larger than Milwaukee, and so more challenging she thought.

She and her friend (and cousin) Mary Walsh, four years older, who lived on a neighboring farm, talked about what life in Chicago might be like. Mary needed only a few credits for her teaching certification, so she could afford a semester away with Jessica. Mary was intrigued by the excitement of Chicago, but not on fire for it, as Jessica was. No one was terribly surprised when once again Jessica Powers enlarged her arc of possibilities and moved to Chicago to take up part time residence there during the winter months. She was eighteen and all things seemed possible.

By day she worked at a railroad manufacturing company in the typing pool, lost in the impersonal production line, a "brown cowled cat-tail." By night she was lost in books. Sometimes in her rush to get to the library she would forget to eat, not remembering she needed nutrition, until a fainting spell was imminent. She loved the Chicago crowds and delighted in mingling with them, bracing herself against the sharp winds, a small figure, bent, intent, sometimes unwittingly colliding with the stockbrokers and scions of business. On one occasion she repeatedly blocked the path of a serious pedestrian, seemingly unable to move left or right without running into him. The gentleman took matters into his own hands, lifted Jessica aloft by the shoulders (ever so gently), and placed her unambiguously out of his path.

It was that kind of energy that both pushed her search (always the search) and stayed her to respond, to write, to put down in some way the music that dwelt in Chicago's soul. Michigan Boulevard spoke to her. Coming home alone, especially on snowy or rainy nights, when street lights shone on particles of water, she felt as if she shared the street with Beauty.

The aloneness seemed essential to her experience, but equally essential was the need to speak of it, to give it in some way to another.[6] She wrote

Michigan Boulevard
on a rainy night

I shall love this golden street
Dim with golden blur
Like a road to Beauty's house
Calling me to her.

No one tells which house is hers,
Why or how she came
But I know she walks tonight
Down this street of flame,

Wan and tired and wistful eyed.
Though we'll never meet,
'Tis in youth that once we two
Shared a golden street.[7]

Here we see one of her earliest explicit statements about the centrality of Beauty in her search, a theme that is repeated throughout a life time of poetics.

She spent much of 1923 and 1924 in Chicago. One Sunday afternoon, soon after her arrival, she accompanied a friend, Regina Anglund, to the Dominican Priory located in River Forest on the outskirts of the city. It was newly built to house the young men being formed in the ways of monasticism, according to the tradition of St. Dominic. Regina Anglund could walk only with crutches, the result of a childhood accident. She is remembered though as laughing, fun to be with, as one who minimized her pain and limitations. Jessica's wit and love of jokes were likely companions for Regina's personality.

When Regina introduced Jessica Powers and Christopher Powell they immediately recognized each other as natural allies. Christopher invited Jessica to participate in the novices' "Literary Guild." They were both young (she eighteen and he twenty).

Enamored of poetry, theater and the artistic life, standing firmly in the tradition of Catholic spirituality, their conversation promised each of them a way to probe the nature of reality and a way to explore the phenomenal universe.[8] Jessica regularly participated in the Priory's Literary Guild, visiting Christopher Sunday afternoons for almost two years during her intermittent residence in Chicago, enjoying a kind of salon.

Jessica would bring books of poetry or journals (like *Poetry,* published in Chicago), leave them for Christopher and his friends to read, and then return to discuss them in two weeks. They also read their own poems to one another and received critique from one another in a supportive environment. Sara Teasdale, Carl Sandburg, Countee Cullen and other contemporary poets "joined them" in the parlor, their verses the focus of the young people's creative energies. Jessica had a particular affinity for Countee Cullen, who was about her own age, and whose ironic verses housed the pain of Black Americans. Jessica identified with their servitude. She liked to recite "For A Lady I Know," one of Cullen's lance-like pieces.

Jessica's sense of social concern was alive even at age eighteen, in a way that was authentic for her introverted personality.

Among Christopher's fellow novices and participants in the Guild, was Urban Nagle who later began the Blackfriars Theater in New York.[9]

The Sunday salons at the Priory were not the only joys of Jessica's life in Chicago. Mary Walsh did come from Cat Tail Valley, as they had planned, and was the perfect companion to share the adventure of exploring the city built in the curve of Lake Michigan. Jessica found her friend a filing job at the American Medical Association. After work they were free to take extended walks along the lake shore. These proved to be excursions of the mind as well as of urban nature. When they weren't walking they were in the library where stacks of poetry books awaited appreciative readers like Mary and Jessica. Weekends and evenings often found the two young women settled in a public library reading room. Jessica's role was that of selector, creating for Mary a mountain of literature vast enough for a lifetime of reading. Laughingly, she'd suggest to her friend that the stack of volumes were only "today's program." There'd be more next week!

So much was fun for them, even Sunday Mass. One Sunday morning they climbed to the choir loft in Our Lady of Sorrows Church where they could look out upon the entire congregation and enjoy a wide view of the sanctuary. They were kneeling in the first row of the loft, praying in preparation for Mass, when a well-dressed man entered the nave and strode purposefully to the front. Tucked conspicuously in the belt of the gentleman's cashmere coat was a lady's slip. The choir loft was filled with muffled laughter until another worshipper pointed out to the hastily dressed man his unwitting appendage.

Churches provided more than laughter, they also prodded Jessica's innately contemplative nature. The "Church of Our Lady of Sorrows, Chicago" tells of a moment of deep connectedness with Mary, the mother of Jesus. She enters the church of "Mary's desolation" and finds not a scarred woman, but one whose name was "Morningstar."

> Music walked with her as with harmony
>   And spoke the titles that her nuptials hold:
> Mystical Rose and Tower of Ivory,
>   Ark of the Covenant and House of Gold.

She then asks questions of the mystery that bonds sorrow and ultimate ecstasy.

Her dress was the bright satin of all luster,
  Whiter than moonlight on the whitest snow.
Why did I find her where the bent reeds cluster
  And the shorn lamb driven by wind would go?[10]

Jessica, who referred to herself as a "brown cowled reed" of Cat Tail Valley, was in the presence of Beatitude, and there makes some kind of decisive turn: "Here I am vowed to Light and His bride forever." The poem was published in 1939,[11] some sixteen years after her time in Chicago. The church of Our Lady of Sorrows, like almost all genuine encounters, continued to live in Jessica Powers's soul and imagination, to be born anew, in ordered rhythms and rhymes. The Chicago experience yielded some of her finest lyric poems. Some of them were written later when she had returned to Cat Tail Valley.

In 1924 Jessica showed signs of tuberculosis: fever and enervation. On a few occasions she coughed up blood. Mary Walsh's family was alarmed enough to call her home to Mauston. Jessica consulted Dr. Smyth, known to her family, who said she need not go to a sanitarium; she could be treated on the farm. Once again Jessica packed up, said good-bye to the rush of Chicago and all it offered her restless spirit, and returned to the farm, believing it a temporary separation. She minimized the TB, and was sure she would soon be back on Michigan Boulevard.

It was not until 1882 that the cause of tuberculosis was announced as the presence of a tiny bacillus. Before that time standard medical texts gave the causes as hereditary disposition, unfavorable climate, sedentary indoor life, defective ventilation, deficiency of light and "depressing emotions."[12] The last item on this list was widely accepted. Kafka believed his tuberculosis was an overflow of his mental illness.[13]

In *Illness As Metaphor* Susan Sontag writes that the murky causality of an important illness tends to immerse the illness in significance. That was certainly the case with tuberculosis. For more than a century and a half, TB provided a metamorphic equivalent for delicacy, sensitivity, sadness, powerlessness (61). In the Victorian sensibilities, which dominated Anglo and American culture long after

Queen Victoria and the period itself had run their course, TB was associated with poets, perceived as quintessentially vulnerable. Sontag holds that this particular disease was in the service of a romantic view of the world (69). It was thought to spiritualize consciousness. Artists of various kinds often languished with the disease and helped to popularize its image as situated in the bohemian life, claiming those who were both passionate and repressed (Sontag, 38).

In addition to air and food and rest, travel to a better climate was invented as a treatment for TB, and diverse places were considered equally effective: the south, mountains, deserts, islands. And so we have Keats moving to Rome; Chopin in the islands of the western Mediterranean; D.H. Lawrence roaming over half the globe (Sontag, 33). The point was to escape the city where in the closeness and stimulation of large numbers of people it was believed lurked the seeds of the disease. Escape from the city is exactly what Jessica Powers did not want. Like Lawrence, she could have (and would have) traveled the earth:

> I would have wed a pirate chief,
> had I lived long and long ago,
> and made my home a ship that rides
> wherever winds can blow!
>
> ("Had I Lived Long Ago," xvii)

She would have sailed, making daring songs, but she would have lingered in the cities: Milwaukee and Chicago. And New York. In her heart she wanted New York, the landscape where she believed poets grew in their vision and their craft. She went home to Cat Tail Valley to get better, so she could leave again.

6

Reluctant Farmwoman

Dr. Smyth's advice helped Jessica's condition considerably. At home among the cattails, the pine trees, the purple bluffs, the whip-poor-wills, she rested. Aunt Carrie was on the farm most of the time, helping Delia with the housework and the garden, and Delia's other sisters were frequent visitors. Aunt Aggie never failed to cheer Jessica with her outspoken, down-to-earth ways, a perfect complement to Jessica's own irrepressible humor. In this circle of family, friends and nature, Jessica read and wrote.

In the spring of 1924 one of her poems appeared in *American Poetry Magazine,* a small magazine begun by another Wisconsin poet.[1] It was a first in her young writing career. She had previously published in newspapers, but this acceptance marked a significant step forward, a gentle affirmation of her poetic calling. All in all these months were a kind of gift. She would not have to go the sanitarium; she had time for her work; she could plan for her future. That's what she did through the winter of her twentieth birthday; she thought about her future. Chicago was certainly in the plan. She knew she could get a job there, and she was familiar with all that the city offered, supports that would ready her for her next spiritual and poetic frontier, New York. New York stood out on the horizon of her imagination like the bright city on a hill top. It glistened for her.

Meanwhile, springtime had come to the Valley and that meant baseball. The Cat Tail Valley baseball team always drew a crowd, especially when they played the local Indian team. Jessica's brothers, Johnny and Dan, played with the team, and she and Mary Walsh were usually among the fans, more often than not outfitted with books of poetry which they read aloud to each other during lulls in the game. The impromptu poetry readings were not particularly appreciated by the team, all young men of the valley, well known to Jessica and Mary. "You can read at home, or anywhere," they said, "why here?" The women just laughed and recited a verse or two.[2]

In some ways, time was suspended that summer of 1925. Calvin Coolidge had begun his quiet presidency earlier in the year. He came to office in the midst of an agricultural depression that only seemed to get worse. There was very little to cheer the people of Cat Tail Valley. Still, they managed to find a lightness in everyday living. Jessica and Mary found joy in visiting friends in the valley. They were particularly fond of their neighbors Maria and Liz Curran. Liz was teaching them to knit a sweater, although they were somewhat reluctant students. One late afternoon they were knitting away in the Currans' farmhouse when Liz insisted they stay for supper. Maria was making a large tomato casserole for everyone (the Curran brothers, Fred and Frank were at home). They were all sitting down to the evening meal when other neighbors, Chet and Myrtle Godfrey stopped by for a visit. Liz set two more places, and the friends and neighbors nestled around the small table, elbow to elbow. The next moments are etched clearly in Mary Walsh's memory. Jessica took some of the tomato dish onto her plate and jokingly fed Chet a forkful. When she took a bite for herself she was jostled and the food spilled onto her blouse. She excused herself and went upstairs to the bathroom. When she returned not a trace of the spot remained. Someone at the table exclaimed, "It's a miracle!" And then Jessica revealed the way of the miracle. Her blouse could be easily reversed, and the wet spot was now in the back. Mary remembers an evening of endless laughter. "Jessica had us all in stitches."[3] Perhaps the fashions of the times lightened their burdens, too. The haute couture centers were borrowing styles from men: trousers and short hair cuts. Jessica and Mary would "borrow" their brothers' knickers, and dressed in the fashion of the day; they toured the valley, spirits as high as their spontaneously assembled fashions. Their laughter was contagious and precious.

They talked of tomorrows. Mary knew she would teach and Jessica was equally sure her destiny was to be a writer. They discussed their dreams during evening walks through country lanes. Jessica was feeling stronger in body and in her vocational direction. The publication of her poem "The Poet" by the University of Chicago's magazine (*The Forge*) contributed to the growing confidence.

The summer of 1925 was filled with leisurely exchanges between close friends, punctuated with daytime hunts for wild strawberries and occasional dances at the Petenwell Rock dance hall. Not that Jessica raced to the dances. She had to be coaxed into joining her friends and her brothers who piled into cars for the twenty-five mile drive to the Petenwell reservoir where a huge rock guarded the dance hall like some pre-historic monolith. On her first visit she was hesitant to enter but rather lingered outside for a long while, listening to the music from afar, absorbing the energy of stars and dance rhythms alike, afraid that if she appeared on the dance floor she might break the spell.[4] A year later one of her most singular poems, "Petenwell Rock," revealing a contemplative awareness of immense clarity was published, again in *The Forge*.

> I never shall forget the first gay night
> I came for dancing here;
> out of a long black road there bloomed this bright
> portion of revel, near
> a tall pine-wreathed rock, as certain as a wall.
>
> Out of the night suddenly lights had mellowed
> to warm young gold glistening against a hall
> where dancers swayed like songs, and music bellowed
> its anger against grief, and laughter flying
> fell on my ears like sounded waterfall.
>
> But overhead the whip-poor-wills were crying,
> crowding all loneliness into one cry,
> and a great rock maintained a wise old silence
> lifting its strength into the starlit sky.

O silver loneliness!
O golden laughter!
O grief that only loneliness should last!
Madness will die, and youth will hurry after;
into some shadowed past
dancers will bow like dust, laughter will crumble,
while still beneath the silver of the moon
for loveliness and joy that died too soon
these plaintive birds will cry,
and this tall rock will watch with calm indifference.
holding itself aloof against the sky. (103)

When she composed the poem (probably in early 1926), its themes of grief and loneliness were more than imaginative. Late in the summer of 1925, Delia was stricken with a strangulated hernia and had to be hospitalized. Moderate treatments failed; surgery was needed. It too failed. On September 12, 1925 Delia Trainer Powers died. She was 58 years, 6 months and 2 days.

After her husband's death seven years earlier, Delia had managed to carry on supervision of the farm work, including business transactions.[5] Her death left Johnny (age 24), Dan (age 21) and Jessica (age 20) with the complex burdens of total management. Jessica's future now seemed settled for her, and not the way she had planned. She would remain on the farm, indefinitely, to make a home for her brothers, while they struggled to make a living from the earth during the decline that signaled the approaching Great Depression. As she mourned for her mother, she mourned too her buried dreams. New York and the writing life were gone, perhaps forever. She settled in to the life of a farm woman.

Jessica Powers's later memories of the years on the farm as caretaker of the homestead were that life was difficult, overly busy and depleting of her always fragile energy. The routines of cooking and cleaning and gardening (as she remembered) replaced her beloved activities of reading and writing. Her memories, however, are only partially consistent with the reality of those years, 1925 to 1936. Work was relentless, it is true. The depressed economy of the United States, and indeed of the world, spiraled toward the stock market crash of 1929. The Mauston area, like the rest of the country, tried its best to cope with increased unemployment, bank failures and business disasters. Farmers were not exempt from the cumulative anxieties, yet Jessica was just as determined as her brothers to keep the farms, their only piece of security in an uncertain world. And that meant hard work for all.

But in the early years of the period she also worked at her inner life. She wrote, revised, and published. *The Forge* kept accepting her work, which seemed very focused on loss and loneliness and death, a true echo of the experience of her young life. She was being stripped, it seemed, of every shred of human love. At times the dead seemed her closest neighbors.

> The dead are always talking in their strange way,
> At night when the winds are still, and dew grass
> glistens
> They are saying things that none should ever say,
> And cursed is he who stands at their door and
> listens.
>
> Always they meet in a manner strange to see:
> The crazy, the dead, and the myriad yet unborn.
> And their words are cold as winds from eternity,
> And their eyes are wise, and their faces all forlorn.
>
> The dead are filling the young unborn with talk
> Of wisdom dug from the mines of bitter years;
> They are frightening crazy folk with thoughts that
> walk
> In the cold and dark, and nameless twisting fears.
>
> I often join them when the lights are done,
> And they see the weight of years on my foolish head;
> When I am silent they think I'm a crazy one,
> But when I talk they know that I am dead.[6]

Before she was twenty-one, Jessica Powers had lost sister, father and mother, and her chance to follow her dearest wish. At times she must have felt dead herself. She missed her mother for reasons that went deeper than any thing she fully understood. *Commonweal* published a glimpse of her grief.

Since she is gone,
This spring I cannot bear
To walk beneath the weight of lilac scent
That presses on my nostrils and my heart
With ill intent

Since she is lost
But lately unto me, I am not strong
Enough without the armor of her love
To brave the daggers in a robin's song.
("This Maytime," Commonweal 4:23 [May 26, 1926]:73)

Family strength supported Jessica and her brothers in the years following Delia's death. Jessica's surviving grandmother, Aunty John Powers, was still vibrant, seeming to grow in wisdom and grace as she aged, and as near to the young Powers as the town of Mauston. And the Trainer aunts were very present. For awhile, Aunt Carrie moved into the farmhouse. A woman in her late sixties, she was somewhat limited in her energy but not limited in her ability to teach Jessica some of the skills of the farmwoman. Jessica's notebooks of that period record recipes as well as verses, a mirror of the details that sustained the ebb and flow of daily life.

Aunt Aggie, born Margaret Agnes in 1865, after James Trainer's return from the Civil War, was full of life, considered by many in the family to be the "colorful Trainer." Two years older than Delia she was forthright, articulate, and attractive in many ways. She had married Charles Fuller and moved to Illinois until the circumstances of the marriage forced a divorce, a rare occurrence at that time, especially among Irish Catholics. Aggie returned to Lyndon Station where she was known as much for her hats as for her strong opinions. She was proud of her writer niece, believing that she had special gifts, and urging her to exercise those gifts. And exercise them she did. Over fifty poems were published in the years between 1925 and 1936. The editor of *The Forge*, Sterling North, described her work as capturing the desolate atmosphere of Wisconsin.[7] The adjective was appropriate for all of her work, but North may have been thinking of a particular poem, "Desolate Land" when he chose that word:

The force of the winter wind is spent
In the blasphemy of a sacrament.
It screamed at the bitter fields and said,
"Take ye and eat—the black earth's bread!"

And I had only the thought to stand
And pity the shame of a barren land.

When the jest of the wind began to pall,
It altered the theme of its ritual,
It shrieked at the doors of my house and
said,
"Take ye and eat—her body's bread!"
It cursed in the very devil's mood,
"Take ye and drink—her body's blood!"

A place must be cursed of God, indeed,
Without food or drink, without fruit or
seed!

And because of a wind's sardonic game
I am hiding my shame in a valley's shame.
(*The Forge* 2:4 [Spring, 1927]:14)

Other of the Wisconsin poems are also marked with a sense of journeying to the wellsprings of loneliness and longing, a searing sense of God, known first hand through the experience of absence. In her continuing correspondence with Christopher Powell she shared her verses, handwritten, three or four at a time. She copied the verse of others, too, bits of poems she thought he would like. Occasionally she used a form of calligraphy in her letters, an art form she experimented with from time to time, throughout the course of her entire life.[8] In 1929, Christopher was still in the River Forest Dominican priory and still writing poetry. Jessica was trying to get some of his work published, and she sent to *Poetry* several of his poems, but there is no indication that they were accepted.

By 1931, Christopher Powell had left the Dominicans of his own accord, but the transition was not easy. Following periods of silence he would write to Jessica some of the anguish of his soul. She accepted the unpredictability of her correspondent. "It is always such a surprise to hear from you; a mile beyond hope, when I am half-reconciled to silence, your letter comes. And I am always very grateful for it."[9] She was reading the works of St. Teresa of Avila and St. John of the Cross during this period and offered to Christopher some of the insights which these Carmelite mystics acquired in suffering. She especially was moved by John of the Cross, "enraptured with the beauty of his books," and declaring that "nowhere had I found such delicacy, such frail glowing splendor, as soft as the diffusion of light" and finding in him "living poetry."[10] She read Willa Cather, too, who herself had been carrying on a correspondence in *Commonweal* about the nature of art in general and about her own work in particular. Cather wrote to Michael Williams, a *Commonweal* reviewer, that

> the literary radicals tell us there must be a new kind of poetry. There will be, whenever there is a new poet—a genuine one. The thesis that no one can ever write a noble sonnet on a noble theme without repeating Wordsworth, or a mysteriously lovely lyric without repeating Shelly, is an evasion . . . No fine poet can ever write like another . . . And the themes of true poetry of great poetry will be the same until all the strongest emotional responses have become different—which can hardly occur until the physical body itself has fundamentally changed.[11]

Jessica must have found the Willa Cather commentary an endorsement of her own lyrical work. She sent one of Cather's books to Christopher—a loan—which had to be passed on to Sister Lucille, now in Racine, Wisconsin. Jessica had kept in close touch with Sr. Lucille. They corresponded frequently and Jessica shared with her "precious friend" her feelings about death (Delia was recently gone, and Sr. Lucille had lost someone close to her).

> We live our days more or less for those we love; we share our sorrows and our joys with them, and then when God calls one of them home, life is only a bleak emptiness ahead . . . it's so very difficult to watch our

> loved ones go out the door into Eternity leaving us so utterly alone.

This letter was written December 19, 1925, and Jessica situates her sympathy for Sr. Lucille and her own loss within the feast of Christmas. "I should be very sorry to have you grieving on Christmas. On that day, of all days, one ought to be safe beyond all grief."[12]

Christopher Powell's letters reveal his own literary preferences. He recommended that Jessica read William Butler Yeats (for which he earned her "eternal gratitude"), and the Irish playwright, J. M. Synge. She spoke of Irish poetry as "the delight of my mind." G. K. Chesterton's portrait of St. Francis deeply touched her.

Together they lamented the muse's departure from their lives, although in Jessica's case that assertion is hard to verify. Still, she felt the absence, even as the verses poured forth. She wrote: "Like you, I cannot even attempt to sing; do you suppose someone rubbed out the chalk marks on our gates?" Her muse was recognizable by her "sad white face, her ragged dress, and her wee starved children."[13] Such poverty and strangeness found a home within Jessica, yet she feared that the wandering inspiration might lodge elsewhere. It never did. In her eighties Jessica Powers spoke of the Muse as residing in her subconscious, hidden away, ejecting images into her conscious sphere.[14] But in her twenties, the Muse was personified, a poor woman wandering where she will.

Jessica and Christopher's letters were often about suffering, with Jessica trying to be a companion to her friend, "a Simon of Cyrene to your cross," setting up a situation of mutuality as she shared her own struggle with pain. "It seems that the shaft of sorrow hits a spot never before wounded. I cannot ever remember being 'prepared' for any of the sorrows that came to me. I think that is why they are so intolerable; it takes us so long to defend ourselves. Yet for that very reason, their value is apparent."[15] She inquired if he had given any consideration to contemplative life. Her letters suggest that she was doing some exploring in that direction, too.

Jessica was conscious of being the only female in an essentially male household, even with the aunts in and out. Her friendships with Mary Walsh, now teaching kindergarten in Mauston, and with Allie, who spent much of her time in Mauston, (a bout with tuberculosis being at least partially responsible for this) were, therefore, extremely important. They provided the relief from farm duties, a situation she characterized to Christopher as "prosaic," one which dried up even her love for books.[16] Her friends, then, were a lifeline of sorts. They could coax her into cross country skiing, or a lakeside picnic, or a dance at Petenwell Rock.

Children, too, diverted her from the fatiguing work and constant responsibility. Jessica loved to play with children, her relatives or children on neighboring farms. She could often be found on a Sunday afternoon, swinging with one or two children on a porch swing, reading to them, or in a more dramatic tone, on all fours, moving about the porch with her hair over her eyes, pretending to be a sheep dog. The children were delighted. These front porch Sunday encounters, not infrequently, generated some verses.

Upon my porch sat little Michael
Lifting his small confiding face
To tell me things that he had accomplished,
Startling things that had taken place.

Ten years back or maybe twenty,
Try as I would I could not call them lies:
The friends he shared in his mother's stories,
The life he saw through his father's eyes.[17]

These were the years when she met Ruth Mary Fox, a respected Catholic writer who had introduced her to the great Carmelite mystics and saints, Teresa of Jesus and John of the Cross. Ruth Mary Fox lived in Racine at the same time as Sr. Lucille did. Sr. Lucille arranged a meeting between Jessica and Miss Fox. Many years later, when Jessica had been a Carmelite for sixteen years, she wrote Fox her gratitude. "Have I ever thanked you, Miss Fox, for introducing me to Our Holy Father St. John of the Cross? I still recall that day in your home in Racine when you told me about him. He is the joy of my spiritual life."[18] Ruth Mary Fox is best known for her work on Dante; she taught the great master to undergraduate students in Milwaukee year after year. Jessica, however, confessed to being more stirred by works inspired by Dante than by the original texts. Renderings of St. Francis, as seen through Dante's eyes, especially touched her. Her appreciation for the mysterious beauty of freely chosen poverty was growing within her. As for "pure Dante" she thought that if she had the benefit of instruction (say from Ruth Mary Fox) she, too, would be a follower of the medieval Italian poet.[19] Ruth Mary Fox was to prove influential in Jessica's life in ways unsuspected at their initial meeting.

In 1928, Herbert Hoover campaigned for the presidency of the United States promising that in America there would be "a chicken in every pot," a symbol of contentment and perhaps even a symbol of the return of prosperity. In any case, enough Americans believed him and he succeeded Calvin Coolidge in time to preside over the collapse of the stock market. The Wisconsin farming communities braced for even harder times as they tried to make a living from a generalized agriculture. This was not the romantic poverty of the poor man of Assisi, and undoubtedly it colored Jessica's perception of her own future. She mourned the absence of books available to her; she felt the beauty of Cat Tail Valley "palling," something she attributed to a lack of contrast. "Unless one is starved of soul, the rich food of Beauty becomes tasteless."[20] Still, she responded, in what seems a steady flow of verse, to the natural beauty in which she lived and moved and contemplated. She acceded to ancient wisdom to *observe perpetually*. In particular, she acted on the guidance of Jesus and considered the birds of the air. Pondered them. United with them. Perhaps united, in a timeless moment, with God. She wrote "Robin at Dusk," "Nighthawks Flying," "Whip-poor-wills," "Doves," "Like Kildeers Crying" during this period. They are all true lyric poems filled with a music, reminiscent of the young Robert Schumann who, in his twenties, said his mind, soul and body *vibrated* with melodies and harmonies. These Wisconsin poems vibrate too. But they are also the mirror of a soul embarked on the contemplative path. "Like Kildeers Crying" is a good example:

Tonight I lost my heart's whole sense of you—
I could not find you any way I turned.
Even your swift impetuous words that burned
into my mind were cold and palely blue

with the small death that any frail words meet
within a moment too profound for them.
The dusk was velvet, bending on a stem
like a crushed flower soft and April-sweet.

When suddenly, out where half-lights edge grey air,
a killdeer lifted from a grassy pond,
seeking the shadows of the field beyond,
flying and crying with a wild despair.

I lost you then. My thoughts like killdeers flew
over a bright pond where day was dying;
the dusk held nothing save their lonely crying,
and nothing mattered—neither love nor you. (184)

At age twenty-three or twenty-four Jessica, it would seem, experienced the fullness of nothingness, in the natural surroundings of Cat Tail Valley. It was the same kind of experience described by John of the Cross, a Carmelite friar, who, in the setting of an austere Spanish landscape in the sixteenth century, described the ultimate union with God as "nada" or nothingness. He, too, was in his twenties.

As the daily farm routine stretched into a decade and her situation assumed a posture of permanence, she kept alive within her a small flame of possibility. In one of her unpublished poems of the period she reflected on what "they" (a life of duty?) tell her, and what her heart tells her.

They tell me this is all of life
        It will not matter much
If I can never walk to reach
        The world beyond my touch.

They tell me any sun-drugged land
        Has nothing more to give
But I know well my destiny
        Is not this life I live.[21]

This can be read, of course, on several levels. Considering the spiritual wisdom that was expanding in Jessica's life it probably represented different realities: her destiny as working poet, and her destiny as one totally given to God. Two aspects of the same reality? Yes, if one believes that "poetry can help clarify love's many mysteries,"[22] or that poetry and prayer are natural companions. After a lifetime of continuing clarification, Jessica Powers could say that poetry led her to prayer.[23] And to love with all its mysteries.

The winter of 1935 was one of darkness. She wrote to Christopher that for two weeks there had been no sunlight at all, difficult for her, a woman "responsive to weather in a great degree." But that was not the only darkness. "I have neither tranquil mind nor a beautiful soul," she wrote. But she does have hope. "One of these days a warm wind will blow and the sun will melt the snow, and the lawn turn green—and a moment later the orchard will break into blossom and with wings on my heart I will approach Divine Providence and say again 'Take me, God, and make me over/ Make me sweet as honey clover . . .'"[24]

She had little hint that winter was soon to be over in other ways as well. The following year her brothers both married; their wives came to care for the two farms and Jessica wrote Christopher that she was about to fly away.[25] After a few months in Chicago, she boarded a Greyhound bus for New York City. Her family and friends wondered why and worried how she would manage. She, though, was unconcerned. Her instincts were to press forward.

Part Two

NEW YORK CITY
(1937-1941)

Introduction

Even though New York City comprises five boroughs, stretching from Staten Island to somewhere near the mid-point of Long Island, it is the other island, *Manhattan*, that means New York City to most people. Commercial bustle, financial wizardry, the theater, publishing houses, excellent drinking water, food from every nation on earth, people in great variety and great quantity—these are the treasures of Manhattan. They are the gifts of diverse cultures.

The Dutch were the first to bring Western civilization to the island, but it was a uniquely Dutch brand. By the middle of the seventeenth century they had established a counting house for Indian trade, a church which still exists today as Marble Collegiate Church and a network of schools. The quasi-official religion was Dutch Reformed, but other groups braved the stern Dutch demeanor to widen the spheres of religious influence. The Dutch were not especially pleased with the growing variety of religious expressions. The Quakers were particularly troublesome to the strict minded Peter Stuyvesant, governor of New Amsterdam (Manhattan).

The British succeeded the Dutch as occupants of Manhattan, and on the eve of the American Revolution, New York had passed Boston to become the second city of the colonies, after Philadelphia. New Yorkers thought of the American Revolution as a mild uprising, for it was obvious that the British were enormously successful in the New York area; indeed, New York City was occupied by British forces. In the midst of the Revolution, life went on. Plays were presented at a little theater on John Street; an orchestra performed frequently in Trinity churchyard (in what is now the financial district); students continued their studies; coffee houses and tea rooms were filled. To New Yorkers, the rebels were simply a nuisance. They were, of course, a whole lot more than that. General George Washington's troops eventually regained the territory and the American standard flew over Manhattan. With the success of the Revolution, New York became the first capital of the new republic. George and Martha Washington took up residence on the island. During their one year in New York, the Washingtons lived at #39 Broadway. One of their great enjoyments was evening walks around the Battery where cries of street vendors, selling baked sweet potatoes and pears, oysters and clams and hot corn, filled the air.

Less than a hundred years after the establishment of the United States the streets of New York were filled not only with vendors but with waves of new immigrants. Between 1840 and 1856, three million men, women and children entered through the port of New York. Some of these were Irish who headed West, some for Wisconsin, some for Cat Tail Valley.

While New Yorkers were dumbfounded at the growing masses, they did not pause in the development of their own cultural life. Theaters, opera, public gardens, horse races, libraries, newspapers—all increased, steadily and confidently. By the end of the nineteenth century the favorite cultural enthusiasm was the opera and, with a great deal of ritual, the Metropolitan Opera and the New York Philharmonic Orchestra opened in 1883. The middle and lower classes were not often found in the opera stalls, however. For them, the *theater* was the object of beloved attention. Union square (14th Street and Broadway) was the center of the theatrical district in the late nineteenth century, until slowly, the center moved uptown, finally settling in Times Square.

The late nineteenth century also saw the arrival of the Statue of Liberty in New York harbor. More than a million New Yorkers watched its unveiling in 1886. Thereafter millions more gazed upon the statue with its raised torch as they passed through immigration, hopeful for a new life in a new world.

When Jessica Powers arrived in New York in 1937 the colorful Fiorella La Guardia, affectionately known as the Little Flower was mayor of New York. He was a powerhouse of energy, conversant in many languages, not afraid to take risks. He and New York enjoyed a kind of love affair.

One of the effects of the Great Depression was clusters of shanty towns that had sprung up in New York's Central Park. La Guardia found a way, with federal funds, to give the men of these shanty towns construction work. They built everything: the subway system, public housing, and many of New York's bridges linking the Bronx, Manhattan and Queens. The mayor would not let the Great Depression stifle the vibrancy of his city. The aliveness was not only in the civil, political and cultural spheres, however; there was also a religious excitement. For a few years, Jessica Powers was part of that excitement.[1]

7

New Friends in New York

The bus trip from Chicago to New York City was long—some would call it tedious—but it did not seem so to Jessica Powers. Every mile took her closer to what she sensed, for many years now, to be a crucial site in her total development. She wanted to lead a more spiritual life, and she believed poetry was her path. For that reason she wanted to get closer to literary sources, to the artistic energy that pulsed through New York in the late thirties. With all her heart she believed New York was the place to house, nourish and strengthen her muse. Her Wisconsin family and friends were less enthusiastic and tried to dissuade her with reminders that she was an unsophisticated farm girl with practically no money, little by way of clothes, few contacts, no job. What she did have in great abundance though (and this was recognized by those who loved her) was the confidence that God would take care of her.[1] And furthermore she felt herself not quite so alone as others presumed she was. The Catholic belief in guardian angels—and her "relationship" with her own angel whom she had named Romuald in honor of the saint on whose feast day she was born (February 7th)—provided both enlightenment and protection. She was keenly aware of Romuald's guidance as she moved from Cat Tail Valley to Mauston, from Milwaukee to Chicago, now to New York. Later, after her entrance into the Carmelite Order, she renamed her angel Miriel.[2] But the benign presence who watched over her entrance into New York was Romuald.

In 1937, the year Jessica arrived in New York City, the world was sorely in need of angelic protection and guidance. Two years earlier Adolph Hitler, chancellor of the Third Reich, had denounced the Versailles Treaty's insistence on Germany's disarmament. To underscore his point, Hitler proceeded to increase his army to thirty-six divisions. Other treaties were being violated as well. The German war machine was growing in numbers and strength, unhampered by other countries. The League of Nations had all but collapsed as a political instrument. Serious unrest was evident all over the world. A major factor in this unrest was the Spanish Civil War which effectively divided Europe into fascist and non-fascist camps.[3] Jessica was not unaware of the state of the world and the human toll being exacted. Her poem, "Lament For Spain" which appeared in *Commonweal,* and was featured on the cover, is one example of her deeply felt concern:

> The rains walk down these consecrated aisles,
> wanders in old confessionals, or peers
> into new darkness with blinking tears.
> O mutilated churches of the dead!
> The Son of Man in all these weary miles
> has not one place whereon to lay his head.
>
> High on these walls once hung the crucified,
> bloodless but whole of form and beautiful.
> Now are his limbs maliciously torn wide,
> the face is crushed and open lies the skull
> in new indignities this Christ has died.
>
> Where is the altar and the sacrifice?
> What phantom now sings his dark Mass alone
> offering up to heaven's startled eyes
> a bread and wine of plaster and of stone.
>
> Yet weep not, Spain, for this wrecked ancient
> splendor.
> Though great wounds gape, so terrible and real,
> your grief lies deeper. Underneath the tender
> salve of the centuries these sores will heal.
> Rather, consider how warm flesh can make
> a finer tabernacle for a King

than gold or metal. Even in the wake
ruined cathedrals, still your sorrowing.

If you must weep, then let your wild tears rain
down on your living churches torn apart,
on men and desecrated tabernacles
locked to the Christ or holding him in shackles,
mocked, spit upon, scourged with a wilder pain.
Remember this, O Spain,
in all the blood and tears of your distress,
that the last churches of your land are less
than the lost human heart.

(*Commonweal*, 28:21[Sept. 16, 1938]:523)

Before the Spanish Civil War was over, more than human hearts were lost.

In 1937 Franklin D. Roosevelt had been elected to a second term, and confidence that the citizens of the United States would know something more than a depressed economy was growing. This confidence was felt in agricultural Wisconsin where New Deal legislation had begun to alleviate the hardships of farm life. Mortgage foreclosures abated; farm credit was more available; various forms of subsidy were put in place. The people of Cat Tail Valley could rest a bit easier.

New York City was a little easier, too. Unemployment was still high, but there was a growing belief that American ingenuity would prevail. Jessica's confidence in God and America's confidence in its destiny merged to support her in what could have been a harrowing situation.

Jessica had arranged for temporary housing in New York at Leo House, but she was unfamiliar with the city's transportation system and was basically unsure how to get there. In her plain midwestern clothes, her unadorned speech, her tentative manner, she must have seemed as one dropped from another planet, an alien in need of help, and unwary enough to take it from any source. Suitcase in hand, she began a walk into the Chelsea section of the city. A rather ambling walk, one imagines, drinking in the sights and sounds and smells of this marvel called New York City.

And then, someone, a man, inserts himself into these first moments of absorbing the city. He says she looks lost, that he knows where she might stay, and how she might get a job. She stops. Is it her wit? Her pioneer daring? Her guardian angel? How does she come to say to the articulate, insistent stranger "thank you, I have a place to stay, and I have a job in mind." And then she turns into a public pay phone (which she does not know how to use, but pretends she does), and acts as if she's calling all the important people in her life: landlord, employer, friend. After a few minutes she leaves the phone booth, (the stranger still in view), and walks briskly to a nearby cab. "Is Leo House far?," she asks. The cabbie gestures across the street and down the block. She is, in fact, a few minutes from her destination. Relieved and renewed, she picks up her suitcase and walks down 23rd Street. She is ready for New York, including the unexpected.

Leo House was established in 1889 as a kind of Catholic hospice for immigrants newly arrived in New York and was located originally in the Battery Park area. In the mid 1920s it moved to west 23rd Street. Staffed by the Sisters of St. Agnes, it provided short-term lodging, simple food, a chapel for prayer and worship, and a safe environment while one navigated the paths of the city. Today it still flourishes as a hotel known for its simplicity, excellent home-made breakfasts, Catholic atmosphere (Mass is still celebrated daily), safety, hospitality and good location. In 1937, it was Jessica Powers's first New York home, but for a short time only. Even though the rates were low, her funds were lower. She immediately set about searching the employment section of the newspapers. Her options were limited.

She took a position as companion and housekeeper for two elderly women who lived on the east side of the city. It was the kind of job she initially found entirely compatible to support her real work, her inner work of perception and feeling. New York, in those days, was steeped in the arts, including poetry, much of it experimental, daring attempts to free poetry from the disciplines of rhyme and meter. Religious poetry, obviously not so concerned about defying tradition (anchored, as it were *in* the tradition) was more attuned to the classical, to reliable structures. Being a lyric poet Jessica was comfortable among the traditionalists. As her work became more and more refined, as she continued to successfully wed nature and religious sensibility, she came to exemplify what George Shuster, one of the founding fathers of *Commonweal*, deeply felt, namely that art and religion are not incompatible, as some contended.[4] To demonstrate the alliance of these two expressions of the human soul the Catholic Poetry Society was founded in 1931 by the editors of three of the most prestigious Catholic publications: *America, Commonweal* and *The Catholic World.* With headquarters in New York City, its stated purpose was to promote a Catholic poetic movement and the advance of American art and culture. To achieve these ends, it sought to provide opportunities for poets, critics and those interested in poetry to discuss and critique poetic works. It did so in two ways: through a bi-monthly magazine, *Spirit*, and by means of gatherings, both large and small. Jessica Powers availed herself of all these means, and was in fact one of *Spirit's* early contributors. "Shining Quarry" appeared there in 1934, a poem that seemed particularly suited for the new publication.

Since the luminous great wings of wonder stirred
over me in the twilight I have known
the Holy Spirit is the Poet's Bird.

Since in a wilderness I wandered near
a shining stag, this wisdom is my own:
the Holy Spirit is the Hunter's Deer.

And in the dark in all enchanted lands
I know the Spirit is that Burning Bush
toward which the artist gropes with outstretched
hands.

Upon the waters once and then again
I saw the Spirit in a silver rush
rise like the Quarry of the Fisherman.

Yet this I know: no arrows of desire
can wound Him, nor a bright intrepid spear;
He is not seen by any torch of fire,

nor can they find Him who go wandering far;
His habitat is wonderfully near
in each soul's thicket 'neath its deepest star.

Let those who seek come home through the vain
years
to where the Spirit waits a shining captive.
This is the hunt most worthy of all tears.
Bearing their nets celestial, let them come
and take their Quarry on the fields of rapture
that lie beyond the last gold pendulum. (30)

The Spirit she writes of in her poem was, in fact, rushing through the intellectual and artistic Catholic world during the third decade of the twentieth century, but the *Holy Spirit* as a focus of Catholic devotion, was not yet prominent. One priest even wrote her about his displeasure in seeing the Holy Spirit referred to as "a bird."[5] Her own perceptions, however, presaged the emphasis on the Holy Spirit and the growth of piety associated with the third person of the Trinity that appeared at the time of the Second Vatican Council in the 1960s.

Ruth Mary Fox, herself a poet, who had introduced Jessica to Dante back in Wisconsin was clearly excited about the new poetry organization. She came to New York City with some frequency to visit her sister who was a semi-cloistered nun in the convent of the Cenacle there. The Religious of the Cenacle were "contemplatives in action" and exercised a form of outreach to Catholic laity, especially to women. At the Cenacle of St. Regis in Manhattan, located at 140th Street near the Hudson River, one could find quiet space for thinking, for walking, and for praying; and Mother Fox (Ruth Mary's sister) was available for spiritual conversation.

The Cenacle also offered a schedule of retreats, usually Jesuit led. People with Wisconsin roots seemed to find their way to the Manhattan Cenacle where Mother Fox received them with warm hospitality. Eileen Surles was one.

A Milwaukee native, she too had come east to be part of the energetic artistic atmosphere of New York. Employed at a publishing company, Eileen, like many young working women, lived at a women's residence in Manhattan, a good arrangement offering both security and companions. For Eileen the Cenacle offered more: an atmosphere of silence and space and she treasured this still counterpoint to the bustle and noise of the city. While not yet a Catholic, she visited the Cenacle often. She first heard of the Catholic Poetry Society from Ruth Mary Fox who sent her a membership card and urged her to attend a meeting.

The more intense and productive meetings of the Society were the work groups where eighteen or twenty crafters of poetry would meet to discuss their work, and more importantly to read their poems in progress and receive the critique of their colleagues. Here serious writers received invaluable assistance.

Soon after arriving in New York, Jessica attended her first work group which met at Campion House, a Jesuit residence in the city. She came into the group quietly, a woman more intent on listening than speaking.

John Brunini, editor of *Spirit,* was one of the regulars. So was Clifford Laube, suburban editor of the *New York Times*, who would become an important ally and mentor for Jessica's work. Eileen Surles was there, too, the first night that Jessica was present. Jessica knew about her, that she was from Wisconsin, that she worked in publishing, that she wrote poetry. She even knew where Eileen lived—all thanks to Ruth Mary Fox who, it seems, provided an informal network for Wisconsinites away from home. And now, after this initial contact with the society, Jessica knew what Eileen looked like. The next day—Saturday—about ten in the morning, Eileen awoke to Jessica's urgent knock on her door. As Eileen called out, sat up on her bed, startled, not quite awake, Jessica entered, leaned back against the door, dressed in coat, scarf, and tam, asked Eileen to have lunch with her. She wanted to pick up from last night. She wanted to talk poetry. Eileen had a previous luncheon engagement, but she could meet Jessica afterward.

This rather unorthodox introduction was the beginning of a fruitful friendship that spanned more than half a century, and that was cultivated in unusual circumstances. Both women became cloistered nuns and for half the life of their friendship they never saw one another. They communicated by letter, occasionally, and several times by phone. But during the days of their young womanhood they were together a great deal, absorbing all that New York could offer.

They roamed around libraries and bookshops where they could read until they were sated. And it was all for free. The little money they had they spent in tea rooms, preferring those run by people of other nations. For Jessica people of different nationalities and races were exotic, and lunch in their national atmosphere fed her gypsy spirit as much as her hungry body. They would often seek a table by the window and watch the rest of the world, admitting into their sight the rush of images that New York held. They took ferry rides, a bargain at five cents a round trip. The ocean, never far away in New York, was one of Jessica's loves. She liked to visit one of the several beaches easily accessible by public transportation, and she liked it even more when Eileen was with her. The ferry boat, while not an ocean liner, became that in her imagination. After all, wasn't the East River connected to the Atlantic? She had read that St. Catherine of Siena's image of God was that of an ocean of peace. That seemed right to Jessica.

The friends enjoyed the theater, too, even though their budgets were always meagre. Jessica wrote to a Mauston friend that she loved *Twelfth Night* with Helen Hayes and Maurice Evans but was disappointed with *Cabin in the Sky*.[6]

All of these experiences poured into the poems which Jessica was soon reading before her peers at the Campion House work sessions. Eileen remembers the first time she read a poem. "People saw right away that she was special." And the other poets helped her in practical ways, showing her different forms, demonstrating how she might follow an image all the way through to the end. She was reading and writing (and being published) and she was learning. She was happy.

In addition to the work sessions, the Catholic Poetry Society held large meetings usually in one of the New York hotels several times a year. On such occasions a fairly well known poet, usually one with a religious vision, would lecture and read some of his or her work. Sister Madaleva Wolffe, president of St. Mary's College, Notre Dame was a featured lecturer at the Waldorf Astoria during Jessica's first years in New York. The month was April. Eileen and Jessica had had dinner together in one of their favorite little ethnic places, but for some reason they were in a low mood, both of them, feeling unconnected to the city's high energy. They walked arm-in-arm, enroute to the Waldorf, sadder with every footstep. Suddenly Eileen stopped, turned to Jessica and said "What's wrong with us? We're in New York! We're going to the Waldorf! How many girls in Wisconsin would give their right hand to be here!" The cloud of gloom slowly dissolved, and then—it began to snow! It was snowing in April, and the city began to sparkle and shine. In the distance the Greyhound bus terminal turned on its lights. Suddenly the world looked different. Laughing now, the girls from Wisconsin, revived by familiar weather, hurried on to the Waldorf and a wonderful evening. Jessica carried within her the image of the Greyhound Terminal until it was transformed into poetry.[7]

It was Fifth Avenue and it was April.
  Who could have dreamed such wind and flying snow?
The Terminal gleamed gold far in the distance.
  And then I thought: where truly do we go?

Is it not thus we wander out of time
  Down the white canyons of white whirling air,
Too cold and tired for beauty, and too sad
  To utter secrets that are warm to share?

Some nights were meant for tears and some for
    laughter:
  And some to hold in trust, and some to spend;
But portents were astir that night we sighted
  The terminal that stands at the world's end.
("The Terminal," 134)

New York City's magic had managed to turn Eileen's and Jessica's tears to laughter. But it was not only secular New York that energized them that April night and other days and nights; the "Catholic Revival," spurred by the arrival in New York of the British publishing house, Sheed and Ward, was cause for rejoicing.

8

Around New York's Catholic Revival

The Catholic Revival was both a period of time and a quality of intellectual life between 1920 and 1960 when European Catholics engaged their religious sensibilities with a myriad of worlds: literature, theology, philosophy and the rather generalized world of culture. Leon Bloy, George Bernanos, Francois Mauriac, Sigrid Undset in literature; Jacques Maritain, Gabriel Marcel, Etienne Gilson in philosophy; Romano Guardini and Henri de Lubac in theology. These and others stirred Catholic intellectual waters. Their work was like adrenaline in Catholic culture and academe, even in America. Even in bustling New York. The Catholic Revival appeared there in the 1930s not as a single phenomenon but more like a tapestry with several points of interest, related and yet enjoying a certain uniqueness.

The year 1933, an out-of-sequence Holy Year designated by Pope Pius XI to commemorate nineteen centuries since the death of Jesus, saw the appearance of the Catholic Revival in New York in several guises.[1] One of them was the opening of the New York branch of Sheed & Ward.

Frank Sheed, Australian by birth, journeyed to Britain as a young man in search of his true vocation. A successful law student, Frank Sheed's Sydney family longed to see him a practicing barrister. But Frank knew the spark for law was not within him. Like pilgrims before him, Frank hoped that a long journey would help him discover where the spark might be. Meanwhile, as he pondered his future, he had to support himself in England, and that turned out to be, at first, by selling religious tracts—pamphlets! The work was not too demanding; there was time to think and spare time to wonder. Some of that spare time he gave to the great English occupation of speaking outdoors. Before long Frank Sheed was speaking on streetcorners and in parks, an apologist for Catholicism under the aegis of the Catholic Evidence Guild. It was at the Evidence Guild that Aussie Frank Sheed met the well trained and gifted Mary Josephine Ward (Maisie), a quintessential English Catholic. Although the Wards were, comparatively speaking, recent Catholics having entered the church in the wake of the nineteenth-century Oxford Movement, they were part of the fabric of a total culture, one where scholastic philosophy was as important as the royal family.

In 1925 Maisie Ward, eight years Frank's senior, married her fellow street corner preacher, and together they launched "the word" in new ways: the written form and the spoken form. They *preached* Catholicism and they *printed* new ideas about Catholicism. Clearly, they thrived on new frontiers. It seemed a natural next step, therefore, to open a branch of their English publishing venture in New York. They came to Manhattan prepared to continue their apologetic preaching alongside their publishing. That they did.

Their arrival in New York was informally announced in the Catholic literary circles. The moment was a kind of confirmation that the Gospel message could renew the various institutions of society if it were presented in a relevant fashion. That is exactly what Frank Sheed and Maisie Ward set out to do. After the crates were unpacked and the first speaking tour completed, the Sheed and Ward offices inaugurated Tuesday afternoon teas where writers and other artists could connect, keeping alive individual and communal visions, helping each other to stay in touch with the Gospel.

In a memoir about his parents, Wilfrid Sheed describes the New York offices as "sunnier in every respect than the London branch, which was never more than cozy." There was a light hearted atmosphere throughout, "giggly" according to the younger Sheed. "I was surprised later," he continues, "to learn that Frank had been deeply anxious about money at this time in order to keep his publishing house cavorting . . ."[2] Jessica Powers and Eileen Surles and others from the Catholic Poetry Society were among those grateful for the Sheed and Ward hospitable cavorting.

The Catholic Revival was also evident in the beginnings of a new newspaper. On May 1, 1933 the first issue of *The Catholic Worker* was sold in Union Square: a penny a copy, the same price as today. Dorothy Day, who had been a journalist with left-of-center publications and who became a Catholic after the birth of her daughter, joined her radical support of workers with the principles of Catholic social thought to produce a unique publication. Peter Maurin, the gentle French worker-intellectual, helped her do that. Together they founded a newspaper and a movement dedicated to a practical spirituality based on the works of mercy. A house in the Bowery section of New York was the Worker center, the first House of Hospitality. There the poor and the destitute could find a bed, food, books and evenings of discussion which Peter Maurin called "clarification of thought." The Catholic Worker staff lived as the poor, sharing their want while engendering hope.

It was not long before young artists and writers wanted to publish in *The Catholic Worker*, for little or no money. *The Worker* evidenced a kind of integrity that made it a desirable public forum, priceless in a way. Jessica contributed "The Rag Man" which was not published until 1942, after she had left New York for Carmel. It may have been sent to the Worker while she was still in New York because some correspondence had been underway between Jessica and Dorothy Day. One note, from the cloister, read:

> "Dear Miss Day,
>
> The verse was a gift, of course. Sorry to have delayed the answer. God's blessing on your work —and will you pray for me?"[3]

The poem originated in one of the familiar New York sights. In any one of the city's five boroughs, in the thirties, one could see a wagon pulled by a mule, or sometimes by a horse, with a rag man at the helm, announcing that rags could be bought and sold. The poverty of the man and his wares was so complete that it was fascinating to Jessica:

"The rag man's cry has summits like a song.
Far down the street I hear his music stir:
The shrill unhurried wheels that would prolong
An endless journey, the slow clomp of hoofs,
The cry with spires, with little pointed roofs.
I think of what Teresa said to Jesus,
And how He answered her:

'I go where no one else would dare to venture.
I gather what the angels would not touch.'
O Jew, is the heart's cloth then worth so much
That its soiled scraps would drive Thee to this
buying,

This walking through the streets, this endless crying,
Leading Thy donkey through the fetid slums
Down streets no other rag man ever knew,
Waiting at doors until a sharp voice comes,
'Down from my doorstep, Jew.'

Jesus, when thou hast reached this alleyway,
Stop at the broken door and presently
One will come forth to deal this day with Thee,
One who computes the value of her love
By Thy indignity."[4]

Another vivid and inspiring figure in this tapestry of Catholic renewal arrived in New York in February 1938, the founder of Friendship House, Baroness Catherine de Hueck. She came alone, carrying a suitcase and a typewriter, finding her way to Harlem via the subway, drawn there to continue the work she had begun in Canada on behalf of racial justice.[5]

The Baroness, or the "B," as she was called, was a woman of great personal force. With her heavy Russian accent and Slavic passion, she was a compelling speaker. She could wrap an audience in a net of total attention with the story of her escape from Russia during the Revolution of 1916 and her capture by the Reds who locked her and her husband in a room in Finland, leaving them there to starve. It was at the point of near death that the teenaged Baroness resolved that were she to survive she would dedicate her life to the Christian imperative for justice. She kept her resolve, in different ways, to the end of her life in 1985.

During her New York years one of her great challenges was to confront Fordham University's de facto segregation policy. The challenge was successful; Fordham adopted support for integration. Elsewhere, though, her young, idealistic followers did not have such an easy time. Women and men were threatened and even beaten as they sought to live the vision shared by this unusual woman.[6] .

The Baroness and Dorothy Day, though very different personalities, and with different apostolic emphases, shared a common value base; namely, a personal identification with and insertion into the Gospel. The "B" wanted to find out how Dorothy handled the many problems that went with committed volunteers and with the constant stance of hospitality inherent in their common ethos, especially as lived in the complexity of New York. One can imagine the intensity of their meetings from the following description. ". . . Dorothy and the Baroness lit cigarette after cigarette until the kitchen curled with smoke. The small ashtray grew into a pyramid of dead cigarettes. I began to wonder how they would cope with the overflow."[7] What overflowed even more, of course, was their love for the poor, and their commitment to action.

Joining Sheed and Ward, de Hueck and Day in the New York Catholic Revival were lesser known but still influential men and women who stirred vitality and vision into religious art and lay spirituality. Many of them found a home in the Catholic Poetry Society. Clifford Laube was among them.

Laube's life had the quality of legend about it. The son of a miner who started the first newspaper in Rico, Colorado, the young Laube spent six years of his early life in an orphanage. His mother was in an asylum and his father was unable to care for him. The Sisters of Charity who ran the orphanage provided Catholic formation and primary education but little else because their resources were so meagre. Christmas mornings, for example, were remembered for *breakfast* which was different from all the others throughout the year. On Christmas there were oranges and small candies by each child's place, and bacon and eggs for all. A feast!

At age twelve Laube joined his father on the newspaper, *The Rico Item* and published some early poems in the paper. He enjoyed his position as a "printer's devil," that is, the newspaper's youngest apprentice, but his young mind and heart yearned for more.

He looked at the mighty mountains surrounding him and saw a mightier presence. He wanted to learn more about everything; he wanted more schooling. Defying his father, Cliff Laube struck out on his own for Durango. He was nineteen years old, already an experienced newsman, and now determined to finish high school. He brought with him only his inventiveness, his determination and his pondering spirit. There was no money, no support of any kind. To sustain himself he worked as a porter in a hotel where his duties included cleaning the spittoons. He finished the four year course in three years, with the distinction of class valedictorian. The year was 1913. He was ready to return to *The Rico Item*, still intensely interested in all there was to read and to learn. But along the way politics caught his interest.

In 1916 he became the youngest member of the Colorado Legislature. Journalism more than politics was in his blood, however. Three years later he applied for a job on the *Denver Times* by submitting a sheaf of poems, an unusual application perhaps, except for Clifford Laube. The *Times* editor at the time was Arthur Chapman, author of *Out Where the West Begins.* Chapman not only recognized but valued the unique talent that was Laube's. He hired the young poet as a reporter.

Five years later Laube brought his wife, Dora Elizabeth Weber (a Rico schoolteacher) to Niagara Falls for a belated honeymoon. He decided that was the ideal time to see New York City, and unexpectedly, on the streets of New York he ran into columnist John Chapman son of his *Denver Times* boss. The younger Chapman persuaded Laube to apply for a job on *The New York Daily News* which hired him as a reporter. He later became assistant city editor and Brooklyn editor. In 1929 he joined the staff of *The New York Times*, first as the suburban editor (he covered the Lindberg kidnapping), and finally as the daily national news editor.[8] But the real life of words for him remained in the realm of poetry. And the most interesting story for him was the relationship between Creator and created. It was a love story. He brought that love to his work on *Spirit,* the publication of the Catholic Poetry Society of America. That love filled the cracks and crevices of his life.

When Jessica Powers met Clifford Laube in 1937 it was a moment of true connection. Similar spirits, in the lineage of pioneers, and sustained by the Catholic worldview, they were at the same time searchers and settlers, restless and rooted in the present. Fourteen years her senior, Laube was poetically skilled in ways that Jessica still needed to learn. More importantly, he demonstrated in his being how Catholic faith and art could create a holistic life. He was, it can be argued, a true mentor for her, a successor to Sr. Lucille. Moreover, as with Jessica, his pioneer determination pushed him into ever new discoveries and undertakings.

When book publishers were reluctant to publish his book of poems, he decided to do so himself, and the challenge totally suited his personality. He bought a second-hand printing press, powered with a foot treadle, and thus began the Monastine Press, named for St. Augustine (on whose feast he was born) and for Augustine's mother, St. Monica. The printing of the eighty-four-page book was done four pages at a time for the entire edition of one thousand copies and involved the taking of twenty-six thousand impressions. Laube did his own binding, learning enough in an hour from an old bookbinder at a book fair to be able to turn out a binding job that was called better than professional, and that has lasted for over fifty years. Nor was that all; he embossed the cover (using an embossing press he made from scrap lumber), and illustrated his book—*Crags*—with wood cuts. It was a work of high craft, in both content and presentation. There was talk of a Pulitzer nomination.[9] His book was in process when he and Jessica met, and he was already thinking of the next book. He wanted that next one to be a collection of Jessica Powers's poems.

He knew her work before she ever came to New York, through Catholic periodicals, and *The New York Times* where she had published several poems, one as early as 1936. It was called "Hidden Secrets" and is not found in any of her collected works.

She tries to keep her precious secret hid
In the revealing manner of wild birds
Approach her hidden nest, as once I did
And she will flutter, frightened, though her words
Bewilder you with phrases and pretence
And fly to subjects half a field away
And although heretofore I followed hence,
I mean to stoop and search that grass some day.
(*New York Times*, Oct. 21, 1936)

Laube, who knew how one moved from the ordinariness of nature to the larger truths, found Jessica's poetic movement familiar. Hadn't he written the following lines?

The place ran wild. I came there without quest
    A pensive rambler down an idle road.
But what I found was fire in the breast,. . .
    Ambers of Autumn over fields unmowed.
The farmhouse leaned, a derelict abode,
    The shell of some old dream long dispossessed;
But out beyond the barn a brightness glowed,
    And I, responsive to its strange behest,
Made gentle trespass through the tangled grass
    To where; past ruined plot and tumbled frame,
Crabapple boughs uprose, a leafy mass
    Of reds and saffrons, like a living flame.
Long, long I gazed there, glad that beauty kept
One brave torch burning for a dream that slept.[10]

The Powers-Laube conversations ranged beyond poetic technique to philosophy and to the creative life. Beauty, its nature and its power, claimed their attention. One evening, after a meeting of the Poetry Society, they walked together to Grand Central Station where Laube usually caught his train for home in Richmond Hill, Queens. They were speaking that time of God, of whether God was more truth or goodness or beauty. Jessica held that beauty was the defining attribute—that's why people are attracted to God. Clifford Laube argued that truth is the foundational aspect of God. It was an expansive and intense conversation, as train after train left the station without Laube. When he finally departed Jessica thought to herself, "Here I've kept a married man from his dinner, from his wife and his children just to try to win an argument."[11] But the argument was stimulating; beauty was an inexhaustible subject. And Jessica learned so much from these exchanges.

Clifford Laube enlarged Jessica's concept of the creative life. That life was about more than verse, he said. "I've often thought that the Creator and the thing created have become too far apart in this mechanized age. Things are rubber stamps, machine made; there is no personal touch," he told one interviewer. "Why is a handmade thing always preferred," he asked? "Because it has something of the maker in it; it has been touched and fashioned lovingly by him."[12] That was the real reason he made his own book of poems. It was a *wholly* creative act. Jessica was fascinated. She wanted to see the Monastine Press, to have a visit with the midwife who would help in the birth of her first book, and which was about to deliver Clifford Laube's *Crags*.

One spring evening in 1938 Jessica and Eileen Surles, after an evening meal together, took the train to Richmond Hill. The Monastine Press identification plate greeted them on the front porch of the small, detached house on 103rd Avenue. Jessica noted the large pine tree in the front yard. Wisconsin seemed closer in that moment. They rang the bell and Clifford greeted them, explaining that Dora and the girls had gone to the movies and the two little boys were in bed. The louvered porch where they entered was a wondrous assortment of minerals and crystals, organized in cabinets, each labeled, each arranged so that the natural beauty was evident. Jessica and Eileen walked past the treasures of the mineral world into the small living room. The overriding sense of the place was that it was a receptacle for books. There was a revolving bookcase, for example, and on the radiators which delivered warmth in winter, stood stacks of newspapers, already read, but not yet ready to be discarded. The dining room adjoined the living room, and it, too, contained bookcases filled with very small volumes, mostly of poetry. And there were photos of Colorado, never very far from Laube's memory or imagination. They proceeded down the steps to the cellar—to the press. A silence fell over Jessica as she sat for a few moments in front of the equipment that actually produced something so wonderful as books, and books of poetry at that. She looked carefully and lovingly at everything: the foot treadle, the Garamond type, and nearby the loom for binding the books. Laube could bind about twenty books in an evening, this after a full day's work editing stories about New Jersey. In between he was busy about his parental responsibilities and his Catholic Poetry Society duties. His wife was clearly proud of her unusually energetic and accomplished husband, although she was known to comment that he didn't get enough sleep.[13] Apparently she knew there was nothing she could do about it. It seemed his activity originated in some place deep inside him.

To Jessica, the Monastine Press was one more bright jewel in New York's splendor. Still, an ambivalence about the city dogged her. Money seemed the source of her questioning. She wrote Christopher Powell that in New York "the spirit matters not at all. . . One looks at the tall buildings and the marvels of modern creation and thinks in a crooked line of the dollar sign." Wisconsin was different, she believed. "Once in a while," she wrote, "I have an intense nostalgic mood when I think of Wisconsin, and the little valley where I lived—where human contacts are not measured by profit." She returned to her valley in the summertime, "to see my hills and pine trees and marshes, and to hear my whippoorwills again." Even though she said she could never love New York, in her own words, she "reveled in it."[14] But it was Wisconsin she loved. She was there among the cattails when Clifford Laube's book reached her, in July of 1938. She wrote him right away, on a Sunday morning in a "tranquil spiritual Sunday-after-mass mood." She saw Laube as a "joyful singer," and contrasted his work with her own. "The thing that most amazes me about your poetry is that there is no bitterness and no darkness anywhere," she wrote. "Bob Faber remarked to me the wide difference between your poetry and mine: how your approach to beauty is always the exultant, joyful one, and mine is dark with sorrow." This observation upset her because she said that God's generosity deserved joyful songs. She thought maybe geography was the decisive influence. "You were reared in an atmosphere of mountain tops and waterfalls and tall magnificent trees, no wonder your melodies are all larksong," she wrote Laube. "And I, instead, had marshes and reeds, and twisted pine trees, and the whippoorwills—can I be blamed that I copied their music?" And then she dismisses place as the reason. "Mr. Faber reminded me that even when we sing of New York you see the splendor of the towers, and I see the darkness and the sadness."[15]

Laube, in fact, did celebrate human ingenuity that created technology as yet another reflection of the Creator of all.[16] He thought New York City was, in itself, a markedly creative act, full of potential. His poem, "Manhattan Turrets" is a good example of his regard for the city:

Ah, surely they were Gothic fires
That forged this steel and edged these spires,
Else how with such an eager thrust
Could they dare upward from the dust?

Yet of these turrets not one tells
The gospel of those great glad bells
That once made Gothic arch and truss
Momentous with the Angelus!

See how cathedral lights and shades
Prism these office palisades!
This towered town will yet breed men
To wake the Gothic soul again.

(*Crags*, 47)

Clifford Laube's imagination and spirit moved easily between the crags of Colorado and the constructed crags of Manhattan. Not so with Jessica Powers. She was less optimistic about discovering something of Wisconsin in the caverns of New York, except through the door way of her imagination. An unpublished poem, "Spell Against New York," contrasts with Laube's confidence:

I have a weapon against loneliness
In this great city that is strange to me
It is my childhood game of make-believe
Filched from the years in my necessity.

I think: if I should open this dark door
I could step into a roadway lined with clover
Take the wind's merchandise of down and scent,
And have the whole starred sky of home for cover.

I think: this room is strange and new
Lifting this window, leaning on this sill
I could hear for my heart's full consolation
The whippoorwills on a Wisconsin hill.[17]

She writes that she is not covetous of Laube's lovely gift.

> The desirable thing about beauty is that we can find great rapture in it, without any consideration of our own inadequacies. In this vein I have often thought that the beauty of God is more than the love of God. When I think of the love of God, I become aware of my own emptiness of heart; when I think of the goodness of God, I recall my innumerable needs; when I think of the mercy of God, I remember my own failures; but when I think of the beauty of God, I cease to exist at all, I become a living adoration.

But she would adore from a distance, "a shadowy corner where I could look forever upon the unspeakable beauty of God without His ever seeing me, to trouble Himself with the courtesies of hospitality. . ." Finally, she states that she is happy to trust her first volume to the Monastine Press, and when she returns to New York, Wisconsin will be with her, "as lovely in memory as in reality."[18]

Her return to New York was marked by newness: a new home, preparation for her first book, the acceptance of her work in a prestigious secular magazine, and the beginnings of a new direction for her life.

9

Looking for Roots

Jessica had left her position as a companion to the elderly women after several months, and changed gears radically, becoming an "au pair" of sorts to several young children. Children gave her joy. She understood them in a way that only happens at the level of heart and imagination, in a Wordsworthian way. "Ye blessed Creatures, I have heard the call /Ye to each other make; I see/ The heavens laugh with you in your jubilee;/ My heart is at your festival. . ."[1] She loved their spirit of jubilee but what she didn't bargain for was the fatigue attendant on full time child care.

A poetry society friend, Jessie Pegis, noticed the toll that Jessica's new job was taking on her strength. The two Jessicas had known each other, and in fact had corresponded before Jessica Powers came to New York. They had read each other's poetry in *The Milwaukee Sentinel* in a column called "The Percolator." Jessica Powers, always curious about others who bore her name, (she kept a large photo of Jessica Dragonet in her scrapbook), made the initial contact when she arrived in New York. The Pegises were welcoming.

Jessica Corrigan Pegis, called Jessie, was married to Anton Pegis, a philosophy professor who had moved his young family to New York when he accepted a position at Fordham University. Jessie was always trying to fit her writing—short stories as well as poetry—into the relentlessly busy life of homemaker and mother. She approached Jessica with a plan. "If you insist on taking care of children, why don't you move in with us and take care of mine? We'll organize our days so we both have time for writing." The Pegises had two children, Charles and Richard, and a third was on the way. It was the perfect solution. Jessica Powers moved to Tuckahoe.

Jessica wrote to Sr. Lucille about the new arrangement. "Everything is going well with me. It is a happy life here with the Pegises. The new baby has not yet arrived though it is almost a month overdue, and I feel sorry for Jessie struggling along through the weary days."[3] She had some other good news for Sr. Lucille too: she had joined the Third Order of St. Francis, and this gave her a structure for her devotional life.[4] Three months later, in May, she wrote, again to Sr. Lucille, that Tuckahoe was enjoying a beautiful springtime; the new baby, Sylvia, was thriving (thirteen pounds and healthy); she (Jessica) was managing to get to New York every week, often to see Eileen Surles. "We have dinner together. . . and we have the most amusing evenings." Eileen spent holidays and an occasional weekend in Tuckahoe.

Jessica was writing a good deal, stories and book reviews as well as poetry, but she thought she "should be doing better for the amount of work done." Even though her work was selling, she was somewhat dissatisfied with the quality. "Every once in a while I remember what Harriet Monroe said. 'It is better to be a good pickle merchant than a poor poet,' and I am almost on the point of learning the pickle business. That sounds a little sour, doesn't it?"[5]

Life in Tuckahoe had the quality of community. The two friends arranged their days so that one of them cared for the children in the morning, the other in the afternoon. This allowed Jessie and Jessica uninterrupted blocks of time for their writing. Housework and cooking were shared. Anton—Tony—frequently invited friends and colleagues from the Catholic intellectual world, particularly the spheres of philosophy and theology, to their home, opening yet another door for Jessica. She listened and learned in much the same way that she had when her father and his friends talked politics back in Cat Tail Valley. There was a difference, however. Tony liked to discuss the religious content in Jessica's poetry, thereby offering her something previously lacking, a theological critique. She had been working on a poem she called "Intimation of Doom." Her planned last line was "Goodness always triumphs in the end." Tony said patiently, "It doesn't. Think about it." The argument ended with Jessica changing the line to "Goodness does not always triumph this side of death."[6] When the poem appeared in her second book, *Place of Splendor,* it read:

> There is a glitter of terror on the world,
> The brightness of the leaves before a storm.
> The sun of this weird day has run to cover.
> Silence of wind gives deafening alarm.
> Something more terrible than death goes over.
>
> What is this wingedness of dark that dips
> Out of Apocalypse?
>
> Faces are lifted to a saffron sky.
> What will rain down? The cowed earth holds
> its breath.
> And each man knows what he would not repeat
> In the last sound-proof cell of his retreat:
> That good does not invariably triumph
> This side of death. (33)

There were many such sessions. Tony, a brilliant teacher, offered criticism as a gift which she accepted, sometimes reluctantly. She often became attached to her poems, and to make a change upset her. But she would usually yield.[7] Always her poems had been explored in terms of the image the feeling, the technique. This was different, and it was both challenging and stimulating.

There were books in the Pegis household, great numbers of books. The presence of a house library was a gift to Jessica. She still frequented public libraries, but a home library was different. At home one could linger over a book for a long time, savoring it. She was reading Hopkins and Chesterton again, and was yearning to learn French so that she might dip further into Tony's collection.[8]

What intrigued her more than anything, however, were the children. Baby Sylvia was heart winning as only babies can be, but Richard filled her life in a special way. He could talk a little, walk a little and play a lot. Jessica would pile up pillows and call them mountains, and she and Richard would mountain climb. Tuckahoe echoed with their laughter, and with Jessie's, when she came upon them engrossed in their fantasy. Jessica loved to study Richard, his moods and his responses. She wrote a poem for him, originally called "Baby Wisdom, for Richard," later revised to "For Richard, Aged One."[9]

> You have your wooly dog, your
> rubber dolly,
> The endless marvels of a colored cart,
> And this whole magazine for
> your destruction,
> Why do you want my heart?
>
> Storm clouds across your tiny
> features threaten
> Soon will your face be all convulsed
> with rain,
> But if I stoop to put my arms
> around you
> The sun in miniature will
> shine again.
>
> How young you are to come
> upon the wisdom
> That must some moment in
> each heart take root:
> No toy of time, no wealth, no
> wreath of laurel
> Can be love's substitute.

Because of the similarity in the women's names, Richard called Jessica "Jea" and his mother was Je-ei. The nicknames stuck. Within the family circle, Jessica was Jea and Jessie was Je-ei. Richard's world was near perfect. No one had a playmate like Jea, who could take words and mold them into a wonderful rhyme for his delight.

In 1939 the Pegis family, including Jessica, moved to Scarsdale. That summer they all went to the beach. Jessica fell in love with the ocean and all its attendant life. She wrote a number of verses inspired by sharing the ocean experience with the Pegis children but intended for *all* children which she called *Songs at the Seashore.* They are humorous and wry. An example is "The Gull":

Oh, see that funny looking gull
Out there beside a jetty.
No one could call him beautiful
Nor even call him pretty.

He walks as if his feet were lead
Or stands and stares about him.
The tiny sand birds race, instead.
Here we could do without him.

But when he sails high on a breeze
He is so lovely, I
Advise him, if he wants to please,
To stay up in the sky![10]

Others besides Richard appreciated Jessica's gift for connecting with the imagination of children. Mother Bolton of the Cenacle was compiling materials for the religious education of young children and she asked Jessica to help with the project. She had in mind a book that would convey the truths of the Catholic faith, particularly the spiritual truths, in language accessible to the very young. An artist already had been secured for the book, and Jessica—so Mother Bolton hoped—would create rhymes in the language that children loved. Jessica agreed and wrote about the reality of children's every day lives for the project asking such questions as "Can spinach ever write to you?" The book, *God's Hour In The Nursery,* was published by the Cenacle in 1947. Jessica Powers requested that her name not appear on it. She also asked that her payment be a weekend retreat.[11]

Her young niece, Maureen (John's child), inspired a more traditional Powers poem, "At Evening With A Child," written for inclusion in her first volume of poems. During her occasional visits home, Jessica stayed part of the time with her brother John. She and Maureen would often walk to the mailbox; the early evening walk was for Jessica a moment of contemplation:

We walk along a road
at the day's end, a little child and I,

and she points out a bird, a tree, a toad,
a stretch of colored sky.

She knows no single word
but "Ah" (with which all poems must commence,
at least in the heart's heart), and I am stirred
by her glad eloquence.

Her feet are yet unsure
of their new task; her language limited,
but her eyes see the earth in joy secure.
And it is time I said:

Let the proud walls come down!
Let the cold monarchy be taken over!
I give my keys to rust, and I disown
castles of stone for ambushed roads in clover.

All the vast kingdoms that I could attain
are less to me than that the dusk is mild
and that I walk along a country lane
at evening with a child. (140)

Jessica was always busy with verses, her "songs." They took many forms. She kept a notebook with verses written to St. Francis and St. Therese of Lisieux, and ideas for short stories as well. She even composed her own greeting cards for Christmas, birthdays and other holidays. A New Year greeting sent to Mauston friends reads:

May you have reprints of old joy
Editions of good cheer
And volumes of success between
The bookends of this year.

One of her notebooks she christened "The Wastebasket: Unpublished Poetry Ancient and Modern, Good, Bad and Awful." She had begun "The Wastebasket" during her last years on the farm entering there the few rejects she received as well as her "fun poems," those written for family and friends, and those not ready to be submitted to publishers. A topical greeting, again sent to Mauston in 1939, reads:

Il Duce wants some colonies
And Hitler wants the Czechs

But you're the only thing on earth
I'm longing to annex.

Dominant in 1939, however, was the publication of her first book of poetry, *The Lantern Burns,* published by Clifford Laube's Monastine Press. It was the second in a planned series that would include volumes from Francis McGuire and Theodore Maynard. Jessica Powers was the only woman poet represented in the dozen or more writers. Together Jessica and Laube selected the contents, many of which had been previously published. The first poem, "Night of Storm," reads like her signature.

The times are winter. Thus a poet signed
Our frosty fate. Life is a night of snow.
Man sees no path before him, nor behind;
His faithless footprints from his own heels blow.
Where can an exile out of heaven go,
With murk and terror in a trackless place
And stinging bees swept down upon his face?

Or what is else? There is your world within.
And now the soul is supplicant: O most
Wretched and blind, come home! Where love has been
Burns the great lantern of the Holy Ghost.
Here in His light, review your world of frost:
A drifting miracle! What had been night
Reels with unending eucharists of light. (36)

Although some of her poems had appeared in an anthology, *Poetry Out of Wisconsin* edited by August Derleth and Raymond Larsson, this was different. She alerted her "kith and kin" as she referred to family and friends about her book's imminent appearance. And she wrote to the respected August Derleth, first about *Poetry out of Wisconsin.*

> Wisconsin will remain my home in spirit; I am devoted to her Dark Rosaleen beauty. And yet it is not actually 'Dark Rosaleen' is it? For there is a richer darker desolation than those words convey. It is the only place (yet visited) to which I could apply both the adjectives *rich* and *desolate,* each in a superlative . . ."

She wrote to him again, this time about his novel *Wind Over Wisconsin* saying, "I am so happy you have done this lovely thing for Wisconsin."[12]

During one of her summer visits to Wisconsin, Jessica managed to get to Derleth's home, a house he built with the money received from a Guggenheim Fellowship in 1938. He called his home Place of Hawks. It was designed as much for his reading and writing as it was for eating and sleeping. Four years younger than Jessica, Derleth was already an established writer in a number of different genres. His principal publishers in the thirties and forties were Charles Scribners, and his work was enthusiastically reviewed in *The New Yorker, The New York Times Book Review*, and *The Saturday Review of Literature*. But even though he turned out quantity and quality his works never sold more than 5,000 copies and he sustained himself and Place of Hawks by journalism.[13] Still, he was the acknowledged "first" among Wisconsin writers, considered generous to other writers whose work he admired and an effective champion of new or hitherto neglected talent.[14] Jessica brought her manuscript to be reviewed by the best. Derleth read with great care the collection of forty-three poems, and named the collection *The Lantern Burns,* a rearrangement of a line in the first poem which reads, "Where love has been/ Burns the great lantern of the Holy Ghost."[15] Years later she wrote "For a Lover of Nature" for August Derleth. It is a kind of internal poetic dialogue where she lays before Derleth the truths confirmed for her by her Carmelite experience. As he once did for her, she now shares *her* knowledge with him.

> Your valley trails its beauty through your poems,
> the kindly woods, the wide majestic river.
> Earth is your god—or goddess, you declare,
> mindful of what good time must one day give her
> of all you have. Water and rocks and trees
> hold primal words born out of Genesis.
>
> But Love is older than these.
>
> You lay your hand upon the permanence
> of green embroidered land and miss the truth
> that you are trusting your immortal spirit
> to earth's sad inexperience and youth.

Jessica Powers in High School

Jessica Powers at Marquette University

Marquette University, 1929
when Jessica attended the School of Journalism

Jessica and her mother Delia Trainer Powers

Mary Walsh and Jessica Powers

Mary Walsh and Jessica Powers

Sister Lucille

Alice Keegan, "Allie"

The Powers's House in Cat Tail Valley
Jessica under a beloved pine tree at time
of her entrance to Carmel

Jessica's "Aunt Aggie"
Agnes Trainer Fuller

Jessica Powers
Marquette University
1922-1923

Jessica Powers

Jessica Powers
1941
in Postulant Dress

Jessica Powers, 1988

Sr. Regina Siegfried and Jessica Powers
Editing session for *Selected Poetry of Jessica Powers*

Dolores Leckey, author
Editing session for *Selected Poetry of Jessica Powers*

Centuries made this soil; this rock was lifted
out of the aeons; time could never trace
a path to water's birth or air's inception,
and so, you say, these be your godly grace.
Earth was swept into being with the light—
dear earth, you argue, who will soon be winning
your flesh and bones by a most ancient right.

But Love had no beginning. (165)

When Jessica told Clifford Laube the book's name, he immediately recognized the rightness of it and set about designing a logo for the book jacket, a dove holding a lantern in his beak, both lantern and dove set against a triangular background. It was elegant and eloquent in its simplicity. He also set about composing a biographical note for the jacket. Laube, never careless with words, described Jessica's poetry as "characterized by a profound religious spirit, unfeigned humility and a deep strain of human pity." He goes on, "The accent is sincere, the cadence true to the interior stir. It is these qualities that have won her an audience singularly attentive and not restricted to any single school or shade of opinion."[16] Jessica was not comfortable with the praise. She wrote to Allie about it asking if the note caused a mild case of hysteria, saying that Laube insisted "over all my pleas." She said, "I told him that the people in Mauston who knew me much better than he did would indulge in loud guffaws. . . Wait until I do a few nice messy murders, I told him, and you'll eat your words."[17] Most people agreed with Laube. One reviewer said, "No singer comes to mind who sees heaven in earthly experience more confidently or who speaks of the supernatural with a more unforcedly natural accent."[18]

Laube could turn out about a dozen books at a time (he was still selling *Crags*). The price for the hardcover, beautifully bound volume, *The Lantern Burns*, was $1.50.

New York had not failed Jessica. She was writing ("all the time," she wrote Sr. Lucille) and publishing, not only in religious magazines and journals, and not only with Monastine Press. *The New York Times* published "Richer Berry," a sensory poem with layers of meaning, and portents of her life to come:

Now that the bright red berries lend
color to the June berry tree
my need is urgent to befriend
denial and austerity.

I touch the fruit with lips of wish
and with the fingers of soft words,
and leave them, a delicious dish
in taste and substance to the birds.

From break of bloom till tide of frost
summer has feasts on every hand
spread with no evidence of cost
for any pilgrim to demand.

Yet I can see through wisdom's eyes
how when the first harsh cold begins,
she takes all fruit and merchandise
save what is stored in memory's bins.

No husk, no shell after the rich
full fruit shall dull my later day.
I shall take hunger first, on which
the spirit thrives best, anyway.(94)

She also had two poems accepted by Harper's, "Poet of a Gentler Time" and "Ice Storm," both of them, like "Richer Berry," a signal of her heart's deepest desire.

Beyond her work, Jessica had her friends. She kept up her correspondence with Mary Walsh, Allie, and Christopher Powell. Christopher had apparently been silent for awhile, but she tried to reconnect. "For some reason or other a little verse you had written has been running through my mind lately, though I had almost worn it out, having repeated it so many thousand times in the years-ago when you sent it to me. 'We were underneath a tree. . . Peterkin and I. . . ' It has always been a poem of sheer enchantment to me, and after all these years I still quite love it." She goes on to say that she shared it recently with someone whose criticism of poetry she valued highly, and who responded, "Anything as lovely as that little verse should not be kept from the public—it is a tragedy to hide it." She goes on to say that she will try to market it, should Christopher so wish.[19]

And who was the highly respected critic? Anton Pegis? Clifford Laube? Eileen Surles? Or perhaps Raymond E. F. Larsson?

Raymond E. F. Larsson (who *always* used two middle initials) was a Wisconsinite who worked on a number of newspapers from Wisconsin to Florida. In his early twenties he began to write poems.

Never very far from poverty, Larsson lived for several years in France, returned to the United States in 1928 and settled for awhile in New York City. It was there, in 1932, that he converted to Catholicism. He continued to write poetry and his work was widely admired in New York and elsewhere. One of his devoted readers was the distinguished historian, George Dangerfield, who called Larsson one of the truest poets alive. Of his poetry Dangerfield wrote: "I have been able to experience, from time to time, that rare moment of total astonishment, when each word falls into place, but one cannot for one's life see how it was done. . . Mr. Larsson's poems at their best have this kind of impossibility, which is one of the most wonderful things in the world, one of our deliverers from the muddle in which we live."[20]

Larsson and Jessica Powers met through the Catholic Poetry Society. Close in age (he was born in 1901), Jessica (like Dangerfield) was very fond of his poetry. She also liked him. Eileen Surles recalls that once Jessica had invited him to lunch in Scarsdale, but because the Pegis family was not at home, Eileen decided to remain. A single man and a single woman *alone* in a house, even in mid-day, even if the bond was poetry, was simply not done in 1939.

In any case the friendship between Jessica and Larsson was an enduring one, even at a distance. It was nurtured by poetry, religious sensibility and mutual respect.

For many years she sought his critique and guidance about her poems, sending him entire collections for his commentaries. Were the poems worthy of publication? Particular lines? Images? She invited his critical judgment about everything from whether or not a piece should be included at all to a particular technique employed in a poem. Larsson would write his comments on the manuscript which he then returned to Jessica, (whom he always addressed as Sister Miriam after her entrance to Carmel). "I like this thought," he'd write. Or, "This line does not seem essential." "Essential" was an important category for Larsson, and theological rigor and rightness seemed to be at the heart of what constituted essential. Frequently he would ask pardon for a seeming negative comment. Jessica would write back additional questions, seeking clarification of his previous comments. So the dialogue would go, glosses on a collection of poems not yet a book.

In some respects the relationship was one of opposites. The Larsson correspondence style was flowery, effusive even. His comments about Jessica's poem, "Renunciation," are an example. "Behold, you are beginning to place in your poems the notches in branches, the heaping of stones that mark the way of the contemplator to the goal of the beatified: bravo! proceed—but do not let my remark make you self-conscious, I pray."[21] By contrast, Jessica's writing style, in correspondence as in poetry, was unadorned, straight-forward, a thing of simple beauty. Different as they were, the relationship between Larsson and Jessica Powers lasted until his death sometime after 1962.

Despite her admitted ambivalence Jessica knew that New York was a good place for her to be in the thirties. She had the cultural advantages of the great city to satisfy her hunger for knowledge and beauty. Equally important, she was in a loving family, with children to give her joy, with intellectual stimulation from books and conversation, and with the gift of a soul friend in Jessie. Her feeling of well being was heightened at Christmastime. She confided to Sr. Lucille that she was delighted to celebrate Christmas with the Pegises, that her heart was warmed by it as if it were the very first Christmas. She wishes that "for one moment I could be God and gather the whole world to my heart in a close embrace of love."[22] To Allie, to whom she could always write in a light hearted way, she was overflowing with good wishes, adding "I feel very much inebriated with the Christmas spirit—singular, not plural."[23] But underneath the sense of fulfillment a relentless question was forming. The question was heightened during a retreat at the Cenacle. The question was, what's next?

Eileen, now a Catholic, was spending a great deal of time at the Cenacle and was involved in spinning her own plans. Religious life appealed to her, but as a new convert she was required to wait several years to be sure the motivation was not simply enthusiasm. She and Jessica talked about possibilities for life in a religious community. Jessica said little about herself except that the only community she was attracted to was the Carmelites, but she pointed out she was "too old" (mid-thirties), "too poor," and probably "too weak" (her health was always an issue.) Then the conversation would turn to Eileen who, seven years younger than Jessica, seemed more firmly planted on the path to religious life. Not the Carmelites, though! She would say to Jessica, "I don't understand that *nada* business," and Jessica would laugh, knowing her friend really did understand.

The turning-point retreat was led by Fr. Charles Connors, a Jesuit, learned and witty and as direct as Jessica herself. During a private conversation he asked Jessica if she planned to continue in her rather unrooted way; "drifting," he phrased it. How did she envision her future, he wanted to know? She spoke then of her Carmelite dream and of all the reasons it could never be. He confronted her fatalism. "You'll never know unless you try," he said. "Knock on monastery doors." And so she did. She contacted Carmelite monasteries in Brooklyn and the Bronx; all of them were full, twenty-one being the maximum number of sisters according to the rule of St. Teresa of Avila.[24]

Before disappointment could set in, the unexpected happened. A new monastery had opened in Milwaukee, in her beloved Wisconsin. Five sisters had come from Iowa to establish the Carmel of the Mother of God. Jessica wrote to the prioress, Mother Paula, testing the possibility of "trying out" a Carmelite vocation. Mother Paula, who had been reading Jessica's published poems for years, responded with enthusiasm. So Jessica went home to Wisconsin to try to answer the persistent question: did God want her to be a Carmelite in spite of the obvious obstacles, in spite of the inherent hardships? She did not share her question and the hoped for answer with very many people; the Pegises, of course, and Eileen. But with Christopher, she simply stopped writing. She was equally private, for the moment, with the people of Mauston. One day, though, she asked Mary Walsh, Nellie Harrington and Allie Keegan to go with her to Milwaukee, to the new Carmelite Monastery at 28th and Wells Street. Mary Walsh remembers that "It had rained and there were puddles everywhere, and she slipped a little bit and said, 'If I fell in this puddle and got my face all muddy, do you think they'd take me?' She had us all laughing, even at the door. We were also all teary-eyed, but she wasn't." After awhile she came out again, very quiet, very concentrated, seeming rather far away. It was a subdued journey back to Mauston.[25] The poem "The Variable Heart," which she had written for Eileen who was in the throes of decision making, could have been equally applicable to Jessica:

> This was her heart till now; a milkweed seed
> anchored securely to a wisp of down.
> It had a drifting desultory creed;
> but love remained its verb, remained its noun.
>
> Think how the wind moved and tormented her
> and cast her forth on rock, or arid clay,
> how even the least gust prevented her
> from any constancy save her dismay.
>
> This is a garden; pray the wind may let
> her down in that soil where her roots can move.
> Ask God to hold her till her roots are set
> safe in the windless moment of his love. (127)

The poem was published in *Spirit.* The year was 1940. It was the beginning of her goodbyes and the beginning of a very different life in the garden of Carmel. She wanted no more drifting (if that was what her life had been); she was ready for her roots to set.

Part Three

CARMEL

(1941-1988)

Introduction

At the dawn of the thirteenth century Mt. Carmel in Palestine was host to a number of men who were living the eremitical life by choice, in seclusion and deprivation (by worldly standards), hermits seeking to know God more fully and profoundly. They traced their origins to the prophet Elijah who experienced the mighty power of God on Mt. Carmel, (1 Kings 18:46) and like others before them, sought God in a life of solitude and prayer. Then in the thirteenth century, as the great mendicant movements were underway—Franciscans and Dominicans, in particular—many hermits of Mt. Carmel found their way to Europe, part of the religious wandering of the era.

There had been a long affiliation of women with the Order, and in the late fifteenth century that relationship was formalized when the *Beguines* of Ten Elsen in Guelders were formally received into the order by the Carmelite father general, John Soreth.[1] The year was 1452.

Nearly a hundred years later the most famous Carmelites of all time appeared on the world scene, although their appearance was geographically confined to Spain. Still the effects of their creativity and their adherence to God were felt across time and cultures. Teresa of Avila, a mystic of the first rank, began a reform of Carmelite nuns in 1562, and the friars in 1568 seeking to return them to the spirit of Elijah, the spirit of penance and prayer. She was around forty years of age when she began her work of reform.

A young friar, John of the Cross, also graced with a profound mystic consciousness as well as a piercing poetic imagination, joined her efforts. In 1593 the Carmelites separated into two orders, one with a more active bent, and one dedicated to the vision of Teresa, that of enclosed life and contemplative prayer. The purpose of this counter-cultural life was not so much flight from the world as it was transformation of the world through the gift of the contemplatives' lives to God. Their cloister meant they were veiled in many ways from the outside world. After receiving the Carmelite habit, those outside the cloister could no longer look upon their faces. In fact, contact with the outside world was minimal. The point was that the narrowly drawn boundaries of existence allowed them to go deep into the well of human/divine existence, energies undissipated, vision focused.

Since the Second Vatican Council the rule of life for contemplatives, including the manner of enclosure and the habit to be worn, has been interpreted in different ways by different groups of nuns. At this time convents throughout the world are choosing whether to align themselves with strict interpretation or one adapted to modern times.

Initially, however, it was the original Teresian vision that spread in many directions, coming to America in 1790 when the first convent established in the United States was that of contemplative Carmelites at Port Tobacco in Maryland. Two hundred years later there were 64 carmels in the continental United States, where women dedicated their lives to contemplation.

St. Teresa discerned that thirteen nuns were the maximum number for a cloistered convent (later increased to twenty-one), and so, when vocations exceeded that maximum (or for other reasons as well), it was the custom to send a group of sisters to a new location to "found" a new carmel, if the local church (diocese) was interested. And so it was when the Archdiocese of Milwaukee welcomed five nuns from the Carmelite monastery in Bettendorf, Iowa in November 1940. They came to establish the Carmel of the Mother of God, according to the rule and customs of their holy mother, Teresa.

10

Early Carmel

The garden in which Jessica hoped her heart would take root, the new carmel, was on one level an unlikely accommodation for housing a group of women dedicated to contemplation. Located on Wells Street in the industrial section of Milwaukee near the trolley lines and the railroad, the two-story light gray wooden building was situated in the middle of commerce and noise. Privacy was maintained by means of an eight foot board wall which enclosed the back of the house and the garden, a plot of ground one hundred feet deep. A single word, *Carmel*, was printed in large letters on a sign above the entrance. Opposite the main entrance was another, marked with a plain wooden cross: the chapel where visitors were invited to enter first, or simply to come off the busy street and enter into the silence. The chapel door was open to the public daily, until 6 p.m., except during Sunday Mass. Special permission was required for anyone to attend the Sunday Mass, a common Carmelite custom in the pre-Vatican Council years. Now, in the Mother of God Carmel at least, others join the sisters for daily Mass.

In 1940 the chapel was small, twenty-three by thirteen feet. A tabernacle on the altar was the central focus, but to the right of the altar was a monstrance, a sacred vessel that held the sacrament. It could be viewed by the nuns in their choir which was cut off from public view by a grille. In the chapel was also a large oil painting of the Vision of St. Elias, and a special chair for the archbishop above which was another oil painting of the Mother of God.

Visitors, after leaving the chapel, would go to the other entrance and ring the bell. A signal to enter, and then one saw the turn, a small revolving wooden cylinder with shelves which could take messages back to the Sisters in the Cloister. The turn sister attended to all this. It was her voice one heard first, a greeting of gratitude, "Deo Gratias." People sometimes came to leave food or offerings of money and frequently, requests for prayers. The sister would turn the open side of the small revolving door toward the visitor and receive both gifts and pleas. One heard her voice and saw her activity, but she was hidden. If, however, the visitor had come to see a particular sister then one would be directed to the speakroom located to the left. The speakroom was small, with chairs placed before a large iron grate as wide as the room. Inside the grating was a curtain behind which were black screens which opened and closed like doors. One heard a key turn and a voice say, "Praised be Jesus Christ!" If the visitor were a near relative the doors would be opened, the curtains drawn aside, and the Sister could raise her veil. The Prioress could choose to grant the permission to others, too.

Normally, however, the sister *and* the opening were veiled. Between the turn and the speakroom was the door to the enclosure which Archbishop Moses Kiley of Milwaukee ritually locked on November 24, 1940, separating the cloister from the outside world. On the other side of the door were the kitchen and dining room (refectory), bedrooms (cells), a garden, a laundry, and the nuns' place of worship and prayer (the choir).[1]

Within this simple frame house in Milwaukee Jessica believed she had found the answer to the question that was filling her being. She formally applied for acceptance into the Carmel of the Mother of God in April of 1941. The community voted to accept her, but the Archbishop's approval was needed. Mother Paula was assured it was forthcoming, but the Archbishop was out of town, so there was nothing to do but wait. In the meantime, Mother Paula was taken ill. From the hospital she wrote Jessica that she was convinced of her Carmelite vocation, and that these little obstacles were not unusual. Jessica wrote back of her family's and friend's dismay at her decision. Aunt Aggie in particular—

wonderful, effervescent Aunt Aggie—was "distressed" Jessica wrote to a friend "as I am myself." She continued, "But I feel that I should do it, and am certain I would not be at peace with myself until I tried to fulfill what I thought was my vocation."[2] She hoped her friend will not think the idea "too fantastic," and then adds, "I don't know if I can endure the rigors of the Carmelite life as it is quite austere, but I have a six-month stretch as a Carmelite postulant before I actually join to receive a name and a habit. Then I believe there is a year before Profession. Surely I will know by that time if I am fitted for the life."[3] It is not only Aunt Aggie who is alarmed at her decision, so are most of the "kith and kin" (as she habitually refered to relatives and friends), among them the Pegises.

Jessica had returned to New York to pack her few possessions, and to formally leave New York. The Pegis household was heartbroken. The children couldn't believe she was leaving. Young Charles, a handsome, brilliant, but solemn little boy had learned to laugh in Jessica's presence. Now, he and little Sylvia cried themselves to sleep for many nights. Richard was inconsolable, as was Jessie. She wept for days. Tony tried to comfort her. "I will be your friend, Jessie," he said, which only made her weep more. Jessica's departure was like an aching wound in the family. Later that year the family moved to Toronto where Tony founded the Medieval Institute at St. Michael's College.[4]

Mother Paula understood how one's friends and family might be opposed. "It is a vocation not easily understood, and Carmel is too sublime a vocation to be followed too easily," she wrote. But Mother Paula knew Jessica's steadfastness of purpose, and was confident in the outcome. In lieu of money Jessica's brothers were willing to give shrubs and trees, an offering from the farms, to the Milwaukee carmel, and Mother Paula graciously and gratefully would receive them. Meanwhile she told Jessica, while they await the return of the archbishop, there are things that Jessica can do. She can get her things together for carmel: a plain work basket with thimble, scissors, and whatever materials she may have in the way of fancy work, crochet patterns etc. "I mean if you have them—don't bother getting any." She may bring watercolors, paints, and pencils if she has them and wants to. She will need a brown serge dress, full skirt to the shoe-tops; a cape of the same material, circular and reaching to the waistline with a standing collar; and an apron of the same serge, reaching to the bottom of the skirt and "well around to the sides." And, of course, there's underwear to consider. "Just what you would need for six months, but add two black sateen petticoats, full and long; they can be worn with the habit, too." She is to bring two work aprons, long ones, brown or gray with a bib; towels and wash cloths. Mother Paula adds, "You mentioned your typewriter and books," and the implication is she might bring them if she wants.[5]

On June 24, 1941 Jessica came to Wells Street to stay: "landing day" in Carmelite parlance. Mrs. Riddlestein (mother of her sister-in-law, Margaret, and a Cat Tail Valley neighbor) made her postulant's dress, happy to do something for Jessica's new life. Mary and Allie helped her with her final arrangements. The people of Cat Tail Valley said goodbye to Jessica, wondering if once more she might be pushing the frontier of her life too far, but knowing, too, the strain of determination that coursed through her. Jessica said her farewell in the poem, "Letter of Departure":

> "There is nothing in the valley, or home, or street
> worth turning back for—
> nothing!" you write. O bitter words and true
> to seed the heart and grow this green answer:
> let it be nothing to us that we knew
> streets where the leaves gave sparsely of the sun
> or white small rested houses and the air
> strung with the sounds of living everywhere.
> The mystery of God lies before and beyond us,
> so bright the sight is dark, and if we halt
> to look back once upon the burning city,
> we shall be paralyzed by rage or pity,
> either of which can turn the blood to salt.
>
> We knew too much of the knowable dark world,
> its secret and its sin,
> too little of God. And now we rise to see
> that even our pledges to humanity
> were false, since love must out of Love begin.

Here where we walk the fire-strafed road and thirst
for the great face of love, the blinding vision,
our wills grow steadfast in the heart's decision
to keep the first commandment always first.
We vow that nothing now shall give us cause
to stop and flounder in our tears again,
that nothing—fire or dark or persecution—
or the last human knowledge of all pain—
shall turn us from our goal.

With but the bare necessities of soul—
no cloak or purse or scrip—let us go forth
and up the rocky passes of the earth,
crying, "Lord, Lord," and certain presently
(when in the last recesses of the will
and in the meshes of the intellect
the quivering last sounds of earth are still)
to hear an answer that becomes a call.
Love, the divine, Love, the antiphonal,
speaks only to love,
for only love could learn that liturgy,
since only love is erudite to master
the molten language of eternity. (43)

She came to Wells Street as a homesteader ready to settle in an unknown region, the region of the soul. Like her grandparents before her, she was prepared to give up a great deal in order to be at one with this new land. She was even prepared to give up her writing, forever.

On June 24, 1941 when she entered the monastery, the door to the enclosure was unlocked for her. Two heavily veiled nuns, the prioress, Mother Paula and Sr. Joan, the novice mistress, met her. They escorted her to the choir where they knelt together in prayer, and where Jessica spoke aloud her desire to give her life to God. The sisters drew back their veils, and Jessica began her new life: six months of "learning" as a postulant to be followed by her clothing day, when she would enter the next stage of training, the novitiate. There was much to learn.

Knowing about the rigors of carmel and living the life are different realities. In 1941 the cloistered Carmelites never ate meat, kept a strict fast from September 14th to

Easter, spent eight hours a day in prayer, spoke only during two hours of daily recreation, one hour in mid morning and one in the evening. At Wells Street, which had formerly been a family home, the four bedrooms had been subdivided into eight cells. The floors of the cells were bare, the walls painted ivory. A picture of Our Lady of Mount Carmel was in each cell along with a picture of St. Teresa or St. John of the Cross. The bed consisted of two boards on low wooden trestles, and on the boards was a tick filled with straw and woolen sheets. A table and a chair were also in the cell. And over the bed a large wooden cross without a corpus, a reminder of the Carmelite's life of penance. The dining room—refectory—was equally severe. On either side was a plain table with a bench large enough to accommodate two nuns. In front at right angles to these was a similar table for the Prioress and Sub-Prioress. There were no tablecloths. At each place was a napkin, a water mug, a knife and a wooden fork and spoon. On the Prioress's table was a skull, a reminder of each nun's final destiny. If all of this seemed strange, the strangest of all was the joy that permeated the atmosphere. Jessica's first months were hard but happy.

The only irritant was the street car bell, jingling every fifteen minutes. Her imagination saved her. She pretended that she was on the car, looking at the people and praying for them. The bell ceased to disturb her.[6] And then she became ill, seriously enough to be sent to the state TB sanitarium. It was late fall; the Germans had invaded Russia. The United States had forwarded a one billion dollar lend lease credit to the Soviet Union, but officially the U.S. remained a neutral country as the world braced itself for destruction.

American neutrality ceased on December 7, 1941. It was a Sunday afternoon, and the Washington Redskins football team was about to take the field against the Philadelphia Eagles. A gray Sunday, blustery, one that said, "the times are winter." The stadium was full. Washington workers, army and naval officers (among them twenty-four year old Navy ensign John F. Kennedy), and New Deal politicians filled the stands. Other Americans were listening to the game (or some other game) on their radios. Some were listening to Dorothy Thompson, a popular newspaper pundit, speak about the Nazi menace.

Pat O'Brien of Associated Press was in the press box at Griffith Stadium when he received a message to "keep it short." He thought the reference was to his sports coverage story for the next day, but then the second part of the message came through. "Pearl Harbor bombed." But no announcement was made in the stadium, only calls for Admiral Bland to report to his office, and J. Edgar Hoover, and the Commissioner of the Philippines. Radio fans heard the announcement, but the fans in the stadium did not have radios with them. They enjoyed the game oblivious to the fact that the world had been forever changed. By the end of the first half most of the photographers who had come to cover the game had left, and the generals and the admirals were gone, but it was not until the game was finished that the Redskins crowd learned the news. As they were exiting newsboys held up papers with the headlines, "U.S. At War."[7]

Jessica Powers heard the news on the radio at the state sanitarium not far from Mauston. She wrote to Allie "I just can't believe it." She expects the new registry (military draft) will include the young men of Mauston and Lyndon Station, and that the mothers and wives and sisters will be heartbroken. Then, in a lighter tone, she asked Allie if she plans to join the navy. Mostly she talked about the cottage where she resides with "five girls," all of them on a screened porch, "colder than the Arctic." If she doesn't have a bad lung she was sure that she had "a flaming nose," she wrote. And she thinks that maybe she had TB of the imagination.

The day after Christmas she writes again. "I just got through listening to the Kate Smith hour and it seemed sadder tonight than ever it was, and it almost turned me into a weeper. But I shook off the spell and here I am smiling bravely through my tears." In all her letters from the statesan (sanitarium) there is news of tests and progress, and an optimism about her health, if not the state of the world. With each favorable test she moves to another cottage, and she expresses the hope that she will soon "graduate."

By springtime she was declared well enough to return to the Milwaukee carmel. She wrote Mary Walsh a letter full of gratitude for her constant friendship, and asked her to say a prayer "that I won't repeat this escapade." She expected to receive the habit in April, but confided to Mary that "they might want to be sure about the health angle. It still isn't a definite certainty that I'm rugged enough to be a Carmelite. But one can dream, can't one?"[8]

The dream came true. On April 25, 1942 Jessica Powers received the traditional brown Carmelite habit and the white veil of a novice. Her brothers and their wives were there, and her cousins in religious life, and her friends—as many as could fit into the small chapel—all who had journeyed this far with her: Jessie Pegis, Allie, Mary, and Aunt Aggie (still unconvinced that this was right for Jessica), Sister Lucille, Ruth Mary Fox, and Jessica's faithful godmother, Nellie Harrington. They saw her dressed as a bride, wearing Mother Paula's veil and white satin slippers. They saw her kneel before the open grate between the public chapel and the Sisters' chapel. They prayed as Monsignor Albert Meyer, rector of St. Francis's seminary in Milwaukee said the Mass. They listened as a group of Sisters from another order joined with the cloistered Sisters to sing the ancient Latin hymns, and as the priest said, "Miss Jessica Powers you will henceforth be known as Sister Miriam of the Holy Spirit." Exactly the right name for one whose devotion to the Holy Spirit so marked her poetry, they agreed. They watched and listened as the priest blessed her garments and passed them through the grate, and as she returned clothed as a Carmelite. They watched and listened as she prostrated herself before the altar while the choir sang the Veni Creator.

Immediately following the ceremony family and friends visited Sister Miriam in the speakroom; her face for the moment, unveiled. Over the next three days they returned ladened with cakes and coffee and preserves. Through the grate they exchanged last words, news, shared hopes and prayer requests. The novice may have become instantly Sister Miriam, but in their hearts and in their memories she would always be Jessica. On the fourth day the grille closed and she began her novitiate, her training as a nun in the tradition of the great mystic Teresa of Avila and the great poet, John of the Cross.

Another respected nun-poet, Sister Therese Lentfoehr also of Wisconsin, commemorated this moment in Jessica's life in a poem, "Jessica Takes The Veil," calling the decision "the most perfect poem that she has written." Lentfoehr writes that though they had not met (as yet), there exists an understanding of the soul.

> I know not her face, we have met in darkness only
> On the austere hills of song,
> But I know on what roads she has come to this
> Beautiful morning
> On what rapturous ways she will go that are bitter
> and long.

And though Lentfoehr is not a Carmelite she can well imagine the life Jessica has chosen.

> Each little bird that alights on the sill of Carmel
> Will rest his wings,
> The stars will go begging to peer through her small
> cell window
> To see how a mystic prays and a poet sings.[9]

Therese Lentfoehr, later a close friend of Thomas Merton, corresponded with Jessica over the years and eventually met her in 1960, when Jessica was once again hospitalized with tuberculosis.

Jessica's novitiate took place during the war, but the wall of Carmel kept the news at a distance. There was no radio, as in the sanitarium, and no newspapers. The people of Mauston, however, either wittingly or unwittingly, provided information about the course of human affairs in the cartons of eggs they delivered to the monastery from time to time. It was Jessica who unpacked the cartons, the bottoms of which were lined with newspapers, front pages mostly, sometimes filled with several weeks of news.[10]

That was how she learned details of the death of Franklin D. Roosevelt on April 12, 1945. The papers described how the train brought his body from Georgia to Washington, with people standing along every inch of railroad track, ordinary people mourning their dead president. They stood in the tobacco and corn fields; they stood on city streets, and at small town junctions. Even at 3 a.m. they were out there, holding their children up to see the train that carried his body. They cried, knelt and sang hymns. Jessica read about it as she unpacked the eggs, weeks after President Roosevelt's funeral.

Even though Jessica was prepared to put her poetry aside, her poetic being could not cease to be. Carmel, including its austerities, was making her more of who she already was, an intensely conscious human being. May Sarton wrote of Grace Eliot Dudley ("A World of Light") that "she consciously created her life each day as if she were a poet creating a poem" with implications of "ruthless cutting. . . and constant revision to bring the creation closer to the heart's desire"; the same might be said of Jessica. Her life was now the poem.

She learned that she was rugged enough for the life of Carmel, but everything was harder than she ever imagined. Even prayer. The Carmelite habit with its coarse wool became the metaphor for God in those early years.[11]

> God sits on a chair of darkness in my soul.
> He is God alone, supreme in His majesty.
> I sit at His feet, a child in the dark beside Him:
> my joy is aware of His glance and my sorrow is
> tempted
> to rest on the thought that His face is turned from
> me.
> He is clothed in the robes of His mercy, voluminous
> garments—
> not velvet or silk and affable to the touch,
> but fabric strong for a frantic hand to clutch,
> and I hold to it fast with the fingers of my will.
> Here is my cry of faith, my deep avowal
> to the Divinity that I am dust.
> Here is the loud profession of my trust.
> I need not go abroad
> to the hills of speech or the hinterlands of music
> for a crier to walk in my soul where all is still.
> I have this potent prayer through good or ill:
> here in the dark I clutch the garments of God.
>
> ("The Garments of God," 21)

Those who approach the path of serious prayer, of experiential contact with God, will recognize the advent of the dark night of soul in this poem, a human condition purposefully named by the luminous star of the Carmelites, John of the Cross. But God also provides for glimpses of light along the way. For Jessica that glimpse came in the person of another novice, Mary Louise Medelska.

Two years younger than Jessica, born in 1907 in Chicago, Illinois, the second of two daughters in a Polish family, she was full of life and laughter. Her father died when she was a child, and she developed a close relationship with her mother. She was attracted to a life of prayer in Carmel, but her sense of responsibility to her mother delayed any decision. When her mother died in 1942 she became the second postulant (and novice) in the new carmel of the Mother of God in Milwaukee. She was thirty-five when she entered.

Mary Louise (Sister Mary Bernadette in religion) and Jessica were true friends. Mary Bernadette was practical and energetic, a talented cook who loved to bustle about the kitchen. In the latter years of their life in Carmel, Jessica noted in her journal that on her designated "cooking day," Mary Bernadette did everything for her: prepared a turkey, vegetables, even dessert. Most of all, Mary Bernadette and Jessica clung together during years of confusion and doubt, a vivid description of Aelred's faithful friends, those who have the qualities of loyalty, right intention, discretion, and patience.[12] Sr. Mary Bernadette died eight months after Jessica. They had spent forty-six years in one another's company.

Poetry was another consolation. Mother Grace, who succeeded Mother Paula as prioress, in response to some gentle inquiries from Jessica, determined that it would be all right if she wrote again during these novitiate years, sensing perhaps that poetry and prayer were not all that far apart.[13] During the year Jessica took her final vows, 1946, her second collection of poems was published. Tony Pegis had worked with a publisher to bring the project to fruition, and the result was another small volume of verse, some of it previously published, some of it crafted since her arrival in Carmel. *The Place of Splendor*, took its title from the first poem in the collection, a poem that reflects the rigors of Carmel.

"No soul can view/ Its own geography; love does not live/ In places open and informative. . ." The poem ends with the piercing question, "Child, have none told you? God is in your soul."

There were seventy-three poems in the new volume, many of them reflective of Jessica's most recent experience as a Carmelite novice. One of them is a statement on behalf of those who entered the narrow way of religious life—(Jessica, Thomas Merton, Eileen Surles and countless others)—as a counterpoint (perhaps unconscious) to the aggressive stance of society, even the religious aspects of it. Her poem, "This Generation of War" is a partial explanation for their unconventional choice.

> Now is the moment most acceptable
> To enter the soul's peace, to rise and go
> Into the vast illuminated silence
> Of regions that the saints and mystics know.
>
> Let it be said of us: They found God dwelling
> To which they fled from pain.
> Let it be written on the stones they grant us
> When peace shall deign to walk the earth again.
>
> These found the hidden places of the tempest
> In the soul's fastness in its long sweet lull,
> A generation of the inward vision
> Whose outward glance became intolerable.[14]

She wrote about the war abroad, and the war within, and all the discoveries of Carmel. She put her soul's struggle on paper.

> There is a homelessness, never to be clearly defined.
> It is more than having no place of one's own, no bed or chair.
> It is more than walking in a waste of wind,
> or gleaning the crumbs where someone else has dined,
> or taking a coin for food or clothes to wear.
> The loan of things and the denial of things are possible to bear.

It is more, even, than homelessness of heart,
of being always a stranger at love's side,
of creeping up to a door only to start
at a shrill voice and to plunge back to the wide
dark of one's own obscurity and hide.

It is the homelessness of the soul in the body sown;
it is the loneliness of mystery:
of seeing oneself a leaf, inexplicable and unknown,
cast from an unimaginable tree;
of knowing one's life to be a brief wind blown
down a fissure of time in the rock of eternity.
The artist weeps to wrench this grief from stone;
he pushes his hands through the tangled vines of
music,
but he cannot set it free.

It is the pain of the mystic suddenly thrown
back from the noon of God to the night of his own
humanity.
It is his grief; it is the grief of all those praying
in finite words to an Infinity
Whom, if they saw, they could not comprehend;
Whom they cannot see.
("There is a Homelessness," 86)

The reading public which had welcomed and looked for the poems of Jessica Powers was relieved by the publication of *The Place of Splendor.* "The ruling by which Jessica Powers has been permitted to write and publish her work since she took her final vows. . . is proven a great boon to readers and indeed to poetry itself," wrote a reviewer for *Spirit.* He likened her technique to a tennis game, full of surprises and deftness. The reviewer, familiar with her pre-Carmelite work, raises the caution that her new life with its doctrinal preoccupations might lead her into prose rather than poetry.[15] It was a temptation she faced throughout the rest of her life. In the early 1980s, for example, the poetry editor of *America* where Jessica had published approximately twenty-five poems over the years, began to return her recent ones saying they were more statements than poems. He called them "sermon poems."[16] Six weeks before her death, in the summer of 1988, as she worked with the editors of *Selected Poetry of Jessica Powers*, she exercised a similar critical judgement, asking that poems that sounded "preachy" be excluded.[17]

In a 1959 article entitled, "The Nun As Poet" Thomas McDonnell wrote that gifted and talented women entered religious life, and that religious life in turn provided these poets with a centrality of meaning. About Jessica Powers in particular he likens her early work to Emily Dickinson and believes that she deserved (but did not get) the same critical attention as Louise Bogan and Elizabeth Bishop. He singles out "Counsel for Silence" as a legitimate sonnet and as one that ranks with any written by a woman in this country.[18] Jessica, herself, in the final weeks of her life identified "Counsel for Silence" as a "good poem," a rare commentary on her part.[19] It was published in 1951.

> Go without ceremony of departure
> And shade no subtlest word with your farewell.
> Let the air speak the mystery of your absence
> and the discerning have their minor feast
> On savory possible or probable.
> Seeing the body present, they will wonder
> Where went the secret soul, by then secure
> Out past your grief beside some torrent's pure
> Refreshment. Do not wait to copy down
> the name, much less address, of who might need you.
> Here you are pilgrim with no ties to earth.
> Walk out alone and make the never-told
> Your healing distance and your anchorhold.
> And let the ravens feed you. (85)

Advent and Christmas in Carmel were memorable. To those unfamiliar with monastery customs, the traditions might seem curious or even strange. But for the Carmelites, the customs were part of a heritage, handed on from generation to generation, in the way of strong families. There was a long established devotion to the Infant Jesus. Each carmel had its own special statue of the Infant that was often moved from cell to cell. Each Sister drew a paper (a "billet") saying how little Jesus came to her *this* Advent: as the Gift of the Trinity, or the Joy of God or whatever. On Christmas Eve there was a procession. The nuns dressed in their white mantles (capes) and their veils, carried lighted candles and processed through the monastery to the Prioress's cell, singing a hymn in honor of Mary. Reverend Mother would then take the statue of the Infant Jesus from her cell and carry it to the others, blessing the nuns with the statue. Then all together the nuns would proceed to the Infirmary to visit those sisters too ill to participate. Finally, they arrived at the crib in the Chapter Room (official meeting room). After Midnight Mass and Lauds, the nuns would gather at the crib, singing "Adeste Fideles" and "Canticles of the Infant Jesus," songs they had written about their own devotions to the Infant.[20]

Another Christmas custom was that of "Dancing to Little Jesus." In a spirit of joyful celebration the nuns would dance to songs especially written for Christmas. A sense of childhood seemed to be recaptured during the festive Christmas season. In that spirit, Jessica turned her writing skill to Christmas poems and hymns, and shared them with carmels throughout the country, and with the Carmelite priests and brothers as well. A collection of these Christmas songs was privately published in 1980 under the title, *Journey to Bethlehem.*

Jessica wrote poems for Carmelite sisters, too, much as she had written for her family earlier in her life. She wrote for the novices (as novice mistress she was especially devoted to them), for sisters who were ill, for the entire community. These were labors of love. She wrote Sister Lucille her feelings about the monastery. "We have a lovely community—each Sister different in this vocation like a variety of flowers in Our Lady's garden."[21]

The community was growing in size, beyond the original eight cells. Sheds and hut-like structures in back of the main house were employed to accommodate the overflow. It was clear that a new monastery was needed.

Visitors who came to the speakroom and heard about the crowded conditions agreed. Mary Walsh's brother, Jim, was an optometrist who was admitted to the cloister to examine the nuns' eyes. He was a first-hand witness to their difficult living conditions. He also was a first-hand witness about Jessica's welfare. He reported to the Mauston people that their Jessica was very much the same, a little grayer, but still full of humor. When in December 1954 Jessica Powers was elected prioress her humor served as a valuable resource.

She wrote to Sister Lucille in 1955: "Do you know what has happened to me? It still seems unbelievable. In the December elections I was elected Prioress. And we have a new monastery to build soon!" She asks for prayers "that I survive this triennial," and adds how heartbroken she is to give up the novices who are "gentle and loving and walk the simple ways." Despite the new responsibility she tells Sister Lucille that she is happy. "For a long time my soul has been filled with praise and joy. I think I shall die, someday, of the infinite goodness of God."[22]

11

Middle Years

Carmelites elect their prioress for a three-year term. One may be re-elected, and it is possible to serve for decades, although that is more unusual than usual. That happened in some monasteries, and in some cases it was a good thing. In others it was problematic.

In all cases the election was received as the will of God. Jessica Powers—Sister Miriam of the Holy Spirit—was prioress of the Mother of God monastery for two consecutive terms, encompassing 1955-1961, and a third term, from 1964 to 1968. It was not an office or a responsibility she wanted; it was something she accepted.

The office of prioress is invested with enormous authority, both canonical and moral, more so in previous eras than today, when the style is more collaborative. But during Jessica's terms of service, every decision was laid before her, some of them involving actions that were not only unfamiliar but difficult.

The years immediately preceding the Second Vatican Council were marked by small steps of change for religious communities, including those strictly enclosed like the Carmelites. An unprecedented meeting of representatives from different carmels met in 1955 in Philadelphia. Jessica was present for it. Nuns from other carmels who had known her only through her poetry remember her gentleness; and they remember thinking how shy she seemed. After one evening meal she was asked to read one of her poems. Hesitant at first, she finally stood up to do as she was asked. One nun who was present recalls her own surprise at Jessica's matter-of-fact speech, her lack of drama. "It was as if she did not want to draw attention from the poem to herself," she concluded.[1]

That Philadelphia meeting was a watershed for the nuns. It was the beginning of more direct and personal contact among the various monasteries, and eventually resulted in the formation of an Association of Contemplative Sisters in 1970. The Association helped open the monasteries to the winds of renewal that were coursing through the Church at that time. In its early, preliminary stages it meant more correspondence among the prioresses, creating greater inroads into time, already stretched in a typical Carmelite day. For Jessica it meant a quasi-moratorium on her writing with only a dozen or so new poems appearing during the six years.

An additional responsibility during those years was overseeing the construction of a monastery and arranging for the nuns to move from Milwaukee to their new home. The first task was to find a site.

Carmelite custom did not allow for the prioress Mother Miriam/Jessica Powers to explore alone, or even with one or more nuns, the possible locations for the new monastery. A relative, however, could take them to examine properties. A priest-cousin who was then serving as a pastor, accompanied Jessica as she searched for a new home for the Mother of God Carmel. She and another nun would trudge about, dressed in their heavy wool habits during the hot summer of 1956 with no proper shoes on their feet, but wearing some discarded overshoes as protection against the mud.[2] There were not too many excursions before a gift of land was forthcoming. Mr. and Mrs. Charles Scholl of Pewaukee made an outright gift to the sisters, consisting of seven wooded acres, with a pond fed by a natural spring, and a view of the whole of Pewaukee Lake. It was a valuable gift.

The building plan called for a two story beige brick monastery with cells for twenty-one nuns, additional cells for four sisters who would deal with the public, a kitchen and a refectory, an infirmary and a number of work rooms. Like the Wells Street monastery, and like carmels everywhere, there was to be a public chapel. The sisters had been accumulating funds for the project for a number of years, and they hoped and prayed that some large benefactors would augment their savings. Meanwhile, the nuns made the best of cramped conditions in their Milwaukee monastery, absorbing the noise of the streets and the scatteredness of the makeshift quarters into an already heavily penitential life.

Anyone who has been responsible for a construction project knows how burdensome it can be. It fills one's days and disturbs one's nights. For an introvert like Jessica the burden was even greater. Whatever scrap of discretionary time was left after her duties as prioress—always intensely interpersonal—evaporated. In the years immediately before her election she produced another children's book, *The Little Alphabet*, a whimsical spiritual walk through the letters of the alphabet, with illustrations in the manner of Kate Greenaway's books. Published by the Bruce Publishing Company in Milwaukee, it yielded funds for the new monastery and served as a reminder to Jessica that her creative stream had not dried up, despite the drainage on her energies. It was her last book for seventeen years. Undoubtedly a number of reasons contributed to her literary silence.

The anticipated move may have been a factor. In addition the first signs of change in cloistered life were gradually appearing, and change can be a cause of anxiety. That a few nuns were emotionally fragile is now understood. Then, their instability was puzzling. Comprehensive screening procedures widely used today to ascertain suitability for the cloister were unavailable. Occasionally, therefore, a person was accepted who could not function well in the environment. That seemed to have been the case in the Milwaukee monastery.[3]

Jessica hoped that a new living situation would alleviate the emerging problems. She who had always thrived on sky and trees and birds believed that nature could heal. She never considered herself a leader—she was unsure of how best to deal with troublesome behavior—but she knew that God infused life with surprises. She was hoping the new monastery would surprise her (and the other nuns) with renewed peace. She was determined to maintain some bonds of community in spite of signs of stress. An entry in her journal in 1959 reminds herself that "In our carmel we must *all* be saved," and she, as prioress will make every sacrifice to that end. "Be a little more stripped of treasures of the mind and heart," she writes of herself.[4]

Thousands of miles away, the new Pope John XXIII had just announced his plan to convoke the Church's twenty-first ecumenical council, an event that would profoundly affect every Catholic. Word of the impending Council reached within the monastery walls, although as yet there was no hint as to the degree of change the Council would engender there.

Meanwhile, the central task was to maintain some poise and purpose in the monastery. The rhythms of ordinary Carmelite life helped. There were hermit days, when a sister may spend time alone on the grounds or in her cell, outside the normal routines; there were community retreats, usually conducted by a Carmelite friar (although not exclusively); there was the daily recitation of the offices—the psalms and readings—that anchored the life of the monastery. Still, in a setting that tends to expose every facet of reality even as it sharpens perception, difficulties can be magnified. When the transferral to Pewaukee occurred there was a feeling of apprehension as well as anticipation.

Donations from people like Jessica's dear friend, Allie Keegan, made the move possible. Jessica wrote Allie her gratitude, saying the one hundred dollars would go into the construction and so last for hundreds of years. "I could pick out a place (near the altar, maybe!) and tell myself—Allie Keegan owns this." Her letters to Allie retained the tone of young friends who understood one another even as they grew older.

The Carmel Guild, supporters of the monastery, was another means of raising money on a regular basis. Jessica kept up the correspondence with Guild members, and many of her Mauston friends, with Mary Walsh as a leader, saw that over the years contributions continued and increased.

A year after the community move (October 1959) when the nuns were feeling more settled, Jessica began to cough up blood, a sign that tuberculosis was once again lodged in her lungs. She was admitted to River Pines, a sanitarium at Stevens Point, about seventy miles north of Petenwell Rock, where years before she had danced, and later wrote "Madness will die, and youth will hurry after" ("Patenwell Rock,"

103). She was back in the vicinity of Cat Tail Valley. Was God arranging a rest for her?

At first Jessica was confined to bed. "I can still see her propped up, surrounded by white sheets and reams of white paper," recalls a nurse who attended her.[5] Gone were the old methods of brisk cold and purges to cure the disease. Drug therapy was now available, and that combined with rest hastened recovery. Jessica remained at Stevens Point for one year.

She brought with her a project begun at the Pewaukee monastery, namely the editing of a translation of a French book into English, *The Spiritual Realism of St. Therese of Lisieux* by Father Victor de la Vierge. She satisfied her love for words by laboriously checking every word in a French dictionary.[6] Equally as important she had time to enjoy the natural world. There was a bird feeder at her window, and for hours one day she watched a little female sparrow swaying in the feeder, "peaceful and content, even contemplative." The sparrow was followed by yellow grosbeaks, chickadees and wood ducks. When she wasn't bird watching she was gazing at the Wisconsin River, enjoying reflections of sunlight on the water.[7] Out of her year of river watching, she devised a playful, somewhat free-form poem called "Souvenir, Wisconsin River" (166).

> Mindful of you by love, I think to send you
> token of this enchantment that I see
> when v-shaped sparkles dance on wind-rushed water
> in the sun's path. Insanities of glee
> delight when light here, there and everywhere
> shines, disappears, re-shines—a fantasy
> no words could capture save in small wild fragments
> of   v
> v   v
> v   v   v
> v   v
>   v

This is so very different from any other of her poems. It is as if illness gave her leave to experiment.

She kept up a lively correspondence from River Pines. To Ruth Mary Fox, who wanted to write Jessica's biography, she wrote that she was gathering her family tree and would send it on.[8]

Visitors found her at the sanitarium. One of them was the poet, Sister Therese Lentfoehr, who had earlier written a poem in honor of Jessica's entrance into Carmel. Their visit (and first-time meeting) inspired another poem, "Ballad At Pentecost," with the sub-title *"I visit Jessica Powers at River Pines."* In it the poet likens the sanitarium to a monastery, and Jessica to a true follower of St. Teresa.

> Bound by no canon, trees sift
> sun and cenobite birds to
> the grill of her speakroom, while she
> who with Hopkins had sung of 'winter
> worlds', now startles the day with
>
> summer speech that ricochets
> off her porch wall a flute con-
> certo. 'Here is your tongue of fire.'
> she said as an oriole flamed at
> the screen;. . .[9]

She came home to the Pewaukee monastery in the autumn of 1960. John F. Kennedy, the first Catholic president of the United States, had recently been elected; the Cold War was at its height; the first "sit in" demonstration, inspired by Rev. Martin Luther King Jr., occurred at Greensboro, North Carolina; freedom rides into the deep South followed. In the months ahead Dag Hammarskjold, Secretary General of the United Nations would be killed in an airplane crash in Northern Rhodesia; and Kuwait was about to be admitted to the U.N. Uncertainties were everywhere, and the monastery was not exempt. With Jessica's health still precarious, another term as prioress seemed imprudent at best. Jessica's friend of twenty years, Sr. Mary Bernadette, was elected. Jessica and previous prioresses were available to help. Together they would work on whatever problems arose, and a climate of hopefulness grew within the monastery walls.

Sr. Mary Bernadette's term of office coincided with momentous world events. On October 11, 1962, Pope John

XXIII opened the Second Vatican Council, and every bishop in the world converged on Rome. The first steps in renewal were in the area of liturgy, with the sacraments being celebrated in the language of the people. Suddenly, so it seemed, the words of ritual were in German and Urdu and English. New windows, real and metaphorical, appeared throughout the Church worldwide including the Carmelite enclosure. While monasteries maintained a definable separation from society, the shuttered and curtained grille slowly disappeared. Next the face veils went.

In August 1963 Martin Luther King, who had rallied the civil rights movement following Rosa Park's 1955 stand against segregation,[10] led a "march on Washington." On August 28th a million people filled the Washington, D.C. parkland which surrounds the Lincoln Memorial and extends to the Washington Monument and beyond. Dr. King moved the nation to tears and to hope with his *"I have a dream"* speech. Unity and peace seemed a possible goal. The feeling of well being did not last for long, however. Three months later the streets of Washington once again filled up with people, this time to mourn their slain president. John Kennedy was assassinated on November 22, 1963 in Dallas, Texas. The nation was in shock. The trauma grew as thousands were killed in the escalating Vietnam undeclared war, a policy which deeply divided the nation. A peace movement grew up beside the civil rights movement.

One result of the ongoing ecumenical council in Rome was that the world with its forces and pulls now had access to the cloister, and the cloister to the world. Newspapers were now available. When Jessica once more resumed the duties of prioress—she was elected to a third term in 1964—the monastery and the wider world were trying to deal with the forces of change.

What was she to do about the nuns who did not seem any closer to stability? They were suffering, that much was clear. She thought listening would help. It didn't. It only ate into her scarce resources of time and energy. She was at a loss. The other nuns looked to her for direction, but she was unsure herself about what course was best. She prayed that she could act decisively "for the common good," and she berated herself for her reluctance to do so. She felt she couldn't dismiss the problem nuns. What would they do? Where would they go? They had no money, no training, little formal education. Jessica's suffering was as real as theirs, perhaps more so. How did one get through the day and the night knowing that the next day would be the same as this? If one were Jessica Powers, poetry was a way to serenity and hope. She sent her poem, "Suffering," to the Catholic Poetry Society, and it appeared in *Spirit.*

> All that day long I spent the hours with suffering.
> I woke to find her sitting by my bed.
> She stalked my footsteps while time slowed to
> timeless,
> tortured my sight, came close in what was said.
>
> She asked no more than that, beneath unwelcome,
> I might be mindful of her grant of grace.
> I still can smile, amused, when I remember
> how I surprised her when I kissed her face. (106)

She instinctively knew that suffering, particularly spiritual and emotional suffering, could best be overcome by embracing it. That's how it dissolved.

The experiments undertaken within many religious orders as a result of the Second Vatican Council, especially in the sixties and early seventies, reordered priorities, but not without cost. As enclosure was being reinterpreted, the old ways were mourned by many. Jessica was among the mourners. She agonized over sisters' comings and goings. Was that honoring the rule, she wondered? Where would it all lead? She prayed to God on the silver jubilee of her clothing day (1967) "to clothe me with peace, purity, humility, silence, fidelity, love of others, love of you."[11] Somewhere, in the midst of confusion, out of the cacophony of competing voices, she heard a familiar voice, an echo perhaps from Cat Tail Valley, or from her early years in the cloister.

> Only one voice,
> but it was singing
> and the words danced and as they danced held high—
> oh, with what grace!—their lustrous bowls of joy.
> Even in dark we knew they danced, but we—

none of us—touched the hem of what would happen.
Somewhere around a whirl, swirl, pirouette,
the bowls flew and spilled,
and we were drenched, drenched to the dry bone
in our miserable night.

Only one voice,
but morning lay awake in her bed and listened,
and then was out and racing over the hills
to hear and see.
And water and light and air and the tall trees
and people, young and old, began to hum
the catchy, catchy tune.
And everyone danced, and everyone, everything,
even the last roots of the doddering oak
believed in life. ("Only One Voice," 148)

America accepted the piece "with gratitude that the poems you sent are of such high quality," adding that they hope for more from her.[12] Could they know the cost of such quality? How many more dark nights did she have in her?

Prayers are answered in different ways. For many carmels struggling with renewal, Father Thomas Kilduff, a learned and compassionate Carmelite, was the answer to a prayer. In the years following the Second Vatican Council he devoted his life to helping his contemplative sisters adjust to the profound changes in their way of life. Fr. Kilduff came to Pewaukee and counseled common sense regarding the troubled members of the community. Meanwhile a number of nuns had decided to transfer to other carmels. That seemed to them the path of reason and of common sense. Jessica quietly supported their decisions while asking herself over and over, "where did I fail?" Her answer was that she did not learn to say "no."

Perhaps it was best to try to set down roots in another garden. Jessica considered the possibilities, and had even packed her extra habit, ready to accompany one of the nuns who was transferring to the carmel in Reno, Nevada. At the last minute she couldn't go through with it. "I can't abandon everything," she confided to a friend who believed that Jessica felt accountable to those whose gifts had built the monastery.[13] The year was 1968, the same year that Dr. Martin

Luther King was assassinated with his dream for a reconciled and united America. Pain was everywhere.

The archdiocese of Milwaukee, in the person of the vicar for religious, helped the monastery arrange for the departure of those who were ill. Others completed their transferals to other communities. Familiar calm was restored, but by this time there were only four nuns in the monastery. It was too small to continue. Jessica made some inquiries about how to dissolve the community. Before any definitive steps could be taken, the Carmelite general in Rome arranged for a group of nuns from Albuquerque, New Mexico to join Sr. Elizabeth, Sr. Carol, Sr. Mary Bernadette and Jessica on the hillside overlooking Pewaukee Lake. Once again, the monastery was viable. In 1969 a new prioress, from Albuquerque, was installed.

Jessica may have had herself in mind when she wrote these lines.

> In that least place to which all mercies come
> I find you now, settled in peace, at home,
> poor little one of Yahweh. On your face
> only response of love lies, with no trace
> or drifting hint of what had brought you low.
> Down steps of like unworthiness I go
> weighted with heart (and how heart can oppress!)
> to see you humbled into gentleness
> (and into innocence) so utterly.
> Pray me, blessed, into your company. (111)

The title is "For a Proud Friend, Humbled," but one suspects the poem is a moment of befriending herself.

Was Jessica's assessment of her failure accurate? How does one define a *successful* prioress? Or is the adjective irrelevant? Are the essential qualities in a prioress spiritual knowledge and faith? And love? Jessica Powers served as prioress during one of the most turbulent periods in twentieth-century church history, as well as in contemporary religious life. At times she felt overwhelmed by an avalanche of circumstances beyond her control. Still, she held onto the threads of hope engendered by her faith in God and belief in her own vocation. While societal and church life both reeled under the onslaught of social forces released in mid-century, many men and women reaffirmed their dedication to commitments. Jessica Powers was one.

The archival materials—the chronicles—of this turbulent period in the history of the Mother of God Carmel have been burned.

In the early seventies Jessica's brother John who had moved to Phoenix, Arizona suffered a heart attack. Jessica, who had gone to Arizona for a retreat and some winter warmth, received permission to visit him, and to help.

One facet of the reinterpretation of enclosure was that cloistered nuns could leave the monastery for good reason, of course with the permission of the prioress. Now in her mid sixties it was felt that Jessica's health might benefit from a change to a warmer climate during the winter. Arrangements were made for her to travel west.

On the way she stopped in Chicago to see Sister Margaret Ellen Traxler whom she had come to know years before. Their first meeting had been through the grille with Jessica heavily veiled. Their friendship had deepened as changes in religious life allowed them more contact. Sister Margaret was aware of all that Jessica had been through, and had noted that with every passing year she became smaller and smaller. Jessica was now like the sparrows she so loved.[14]

The Chicago visit was a joyful prelude to Arizona, and to her visits to two other carmels, one in Reno and one in San Diego. Both carmels were peopled by creative and educated women who were shaping contemporary contemplative life. Jessica would have been permanently welcome in either place.

In San Diego she enjoyed days of rest, watching humming birds and purple finches. She made lists of all the trees in California, and practiced her calligraphy. Whole stretches of time were given to poetry, a leisure not hers since her New York days. Victoria Bettencourt, a friend of the Carmelites who had met her bus when she arrived, took her to an art gallery. Jessica loved the paintings and ruminated for months over one, Jean Francois Millet's "Feeding Her Birds," which she termed a biography of peasant children and their mother. With one child in particular she identifies:

> Her peasant childhood motivates my will
> to take my given portion and be still;
>
> or if there must be words, to speak none other
> than: O my Mother God, my God and Mother. (138)

One of the San Diego nuns was a medical doctor, with recognized psychological and spiritual gifts, Sister Desiree. Jessica spent time with her, talking, sharing with her the sadness that never quite left her, a legacy of loss perhaps. Sister Desiree's own work, after her entrance to Carmel at age fifty (she had been on the medical staff of a children's hospital) was to synthesize the major psychological schools with the Carmelite mystics. The result was a dynamic understanding of the genetic, cultural, theological, psychological and spiritual factors in the development of mind and soul. A warm, embracing woman with a Texas accent, she loved jokes (as did Jessica) and she laughed easily. She always appeared to be having a wonderful time simply being alive. The two nuns walked in the beautiful Carmelite rose gardens, enjoying one another's company. Desiree helped Jessica discern between healthy and unhealthy dependency and the relationship between human freedom and love. Above all Desiree understood the workings of an artistic soul, and the value of spiritual mentoring. She believed a prioress was as much a mentor as anything else. Desiree had Jessica record her dreams, and helped her to do her own analysis. The medical difficulties Jessica experienced with her heart while in California seemed as nothing compared to the enlarged capacity for breathing life which she enjoyed there. She was conscious again of learning and growing, although she wrote in her journal that she was still "amazed" at all that had happened, and was still trying to find the truth for herself. When she left San Diego she was certain she would not settle there, beautiful though it was.[15]

She went on to Reno. Her month in that monastery continued the expansion she felt in California. The Reno carmel, high up on a hill, overlooks the city. She described the view in a letter to Allie.

> In the recreation room there are big windows, almost
> the length of the wall, and looking down on the city

> it's like a sea of light. They have only a few tall buildings in Reno so it doesn't have a Broadway look from here—just sparkling light. And the dark mountains in the back . . . I love the mountains and desert country but I love Wisconsin, too. The lake is so pretty there with its changing colors. And the greenness. It must be the Irish in me. The green out here—grass and trees—is often so pale. And dusty.[16]

She enjoyed a kinship with the several artist-nuns. There were paths to hike, and books to read like Maisie Ward's "beautiful" biography of Caryll Houselander. She knew there was a place for her in this carmel, if she wanted.

Springtime came, and she returned to Wisconsin; she felt certain it would be for all her earthly days. She had reached her decision: for better or for worse she would remain in the Mother of God Carmel in Pewaukee. It was where long ago she decided to dig her well, a metaphor for stability.[17] May Sarton says a well is "not a brook in constant motion, rushing down from mountains, bringing all sorts of things along with it . . . The source of the well is deep within the earth. It is fed from within."[18]

The earth for Jessica Powers was Pewaukee. It fed her in ways she did not fully comprehend but she would cultivate and tend it as best she could.

12

Later Carmel

Florida Maxwell Scott, writer and psychotherapist, says that she was surprised at how passionate she felt in old age.[1] One is reminded of William Butler Yeats's lines:

I pray—for fashion's word is out
And prayer comes round again—
That I may seem, though I die old,
A foolish, passionate man.[2]

After her journeys west, Jessica Powers returned to Wisconsin with a renewed passion for her life and her life's work. She was entering into what Eugene Bianci calls "elderhood," one of the final crossroads in life.[3] At age sixty-six, despite some cardiac flare-ups (which she made little of), and the beginnings of osteoporosis, which on a daily basis was more troublesome, she set about the final organization of a little volume of verse to be published by the Reno carmel, *Mountain Sparrow.* The ten poems were illustrated by Sr. Marie Celeste of Reno, who used a variety of print techniques among them silk screen, wood block, and nature block to create the visual experience of these songs. One poem, "The Cedar Tree," previously published in *Commonweal* in 1945, aptly conveyed Jessica's assessment of the time of trial she had recently been through.

In the beginning, in the unbeginning
of endlessness and of eternity,
God saw this tree.
He saw these cedar branches bending low
under the full exhaustion of the snow.

And since He set no wind of day to rising,
this burden of beauty and this burden of cold,
(whether the wood breaks or the branches hold)
must be of His devising.

There is a cedar similarly decked
deep in the winter of my intellect
under the snow, the snow,
the scales of light its limitations tell.

I clasp this thought: from all eternity
God who is good looked down upon this tree
white in the weighted air,
and of another cedar reckoned well.
He knew how much each tree, each twig could bear.
He counted every snowflake as it fell. (176)

She knew that God knew how much she could bear. There had been so many trial testings by this time.

Bianchi argues that the elders among us who enter into the final phases of life actively, "collaborating passionately in the human effort," as Teilhard phrases it,[4] despite the inevitable diminishments of old age, touch into the divine power for developing the world. Engagement, rather than passivity, according to the realities of one's energy store, is the key.

The old have the capacity to image God as the "wounded healer," he writes, because they are the ones who have suffered the wounds of life's stages and whose wisdom has been forged in the "crucible of the world's suffering." Bianchi is persuasive in presenting the aging artist as a model for how to keep elderhood alive for the world. Theirs is not the strenuous energy of youth, full of driving activity and fearful of failure. Rather it is a "subtle dynamism" that stays with the mystery of life.

The elderly artist, at his or her best, has entered into a communion with the joys and sorrows of existence, yielding a beauty not possible in earlier years. One need only recall the radiance of Vladimir Horowitz's piano concert in Moscow in 1986. The Moscow Conservatory was filled to capacity. Horowitz who had left Russia in 1925, a 22 year old from Kiev, was back for the first time in sixty years. As he put his fingers upon the keys to play the first notes of a Scarlatti sonata, a climax of memory and emotion was unleashed. "He played with great subtlety and great power. He gave the crowd pastel rainbows and crashing thunderstorms. By the time he reached the music of the Russian composers Rachmaninoff and Scriabin, many in the audience were weeping."[5] Horowitz was at home, on many levels. The spiritual journey is about going home implies Bianchi. This requires the continued exploration of the inner world, so that ". . . the end of all our exploring/ Will be to arrive where we started."[6]

Jessica was both explorer and settler. At the entrance to old age, the structure of her days was substantially the same as it had been in her forties, fifties and sixties. There was community prayer and prayer alone; her correspondence on behalf of the Carmel Guild which raised money for the monastery; her correspondence with friends; her work assignment which was care for the gardens. "My life is filled with simple, small things" she wrote in her journal. She pruned the grapevine, dug up parsnips, marveled at tulips appearing in late winter. Familiar and well loved routines.

Her journals are filled with notations about the details of a full life. Always there is the weather, a legacy of her farm lineage. Birthdays and anniversaries are noted each year. And Mother's Day. Fifty years after Delia's death she wrote, "I'm thinking of Mama." Phil Quinn, a childhood friend from Cat Tail Valley who had married her brother Dan's widow, Margaret, brought her a box filled with mementoes of her past. The box, she said "awakened long lost memories. A lovely picture of my mother when she was young, a ring and rosary I had in childhood, a card from Aunt Aggie in 1911 (I still recall I used to say to myself over and over what it said on the card: 'Be good and sweet and don't forget Aunt Aggie'." The box also contained her grandmother Powers's bible, and the book of Robert Burns's poems that her Grandfather Trainer brought from Scotland.

Three seasons of the year she would put on an apron and a gardening bonnet and spend hours tending the asparagus bed and carefully picking raspberries. She loved her gardens. She chose to spend the greater part of an unstructured two-week retreat outside in the company of the trees many of which she had planted herself when they first moved to the lakeside setting. She remembered carrying water in pails from the pond nearby to water the spruces. She knew every one personally.

She said this particular retreat was a "search for sacred places in the sun." She read evening prayer from the Carmelite breviary "in the lower orchard amid the white clover." It reminded her of other summers in Cat Tail Valley when she would be in the alfalfa field at evening.[7]

During the summer of 1974, she made a thirty-day retreat concentrating on the prophets Amos, Hosea, Zephaniah, Nahum and Haggai.

At other times she watched the birds and thought about getting a new guide to American wildlife. She and Sr. Mary Bernadette often watched sunsets together in August. They cooked together, too. Jessica loved her friend's desserts.

Several winters she was able to return to Phoenix to be with John and to see other members of the family as well. Sometimes she visited the western carmels which seemed to satisfy her "almost absolute need for light," and where she could practice Zen—sitting and biblical meditation. She tried to learn Chinese during these trips and filled her journals with characters. She also expressed great interest in the Japanese Tea Ceremony.[8]

The Carmelite friars were revising their supplement to the Daily Office in the late seventies and nuns and friars from around the world, musicians and poets, were asked to contribute. Jessica had several hymns and poems in the supplement, and in the hymnal published by the carmel in Long Beach, California. These were under her religious name, Sr. Miriam. The revisions occasioned a good bit of back-and-forth correspondence between Fr. John Sullivan, OCD, who was shepherding the project, and the authors. One hymn by Jessica, "Up the High Mountain" engendered a discussion about the past tense of the verb *to slay*. Jessica solved the problem by using the present tense in the stanza in question.

Up past the steepest
Cliffs of our striving
Up from the deepest
Thickets of pain

Where darkness bound you,
To ravage and slay you,
Till daybreak found you,
Risen again.[9]

Jessica wrote Fr. Sullivan inquiring if a certain priest involved in the revision was "distressed" at the changes. She answered her own query with the comment "Well, we all have little contributions to make to the success of the Supplement, haven't we? And distress might be one of them."[10]

Jessica, herself, was undergoing some additional distress. The changes underway in the Pewaukee monastery—a combination of new people and the effects of the Second Vatican Council—had an unsettling effect on her. The community held many meetings—too many it seemed to her—to discuss how to live the Carmelite vocation. She found the discussions "tedious." There were discussions about what to wear: now the sisters could wear the traditional habit, a modified habit or an ordinary dress. Jessica chose the modified habit.

Someone suggested having Mass in different places. All voted yes except Jessica. (What was a chapel for?)

Television's occasional use for educational purposes and at recreation times was approved by all except Jessica, who thought television irreconcilable with a life of prayer. Furthermore, she plain didn't like it. One journal entry reads, "During recreation saw 'Jesus of Nazareth' on TV; stayed 'till the flight into Egypt, then left."[11] On the other hand, television brought the current world events into the cloister with a new immediacy. No longer did Jessica or the others have to unpack the egg crates from Mauston to know what was happening. Richard Nixon's resignation from the presidency in 1974, the election of Jimmy Carter in 1976, death of Pope Paul VI in 1978, and the election of Pope John Paul I with his sudden death thirty days later, and the election of Pope John Paul II, the first non-Italian in the Church's memory—all this news was instantly available to the nuns. Cloister now had a twentieth-century style mingled with the ancient traditions.

More visitors came, too. There were workshops on everything from feminism ("interesting," thought Jessica), to psychology (which she found "exhausting"). The psychology course required a review of pre-Carmelite life, with peak moments, how one is likely seen by others, how one sees herself—all of which was to be shared in the group. This was in sharp contrast to the traditional Carmelite way of *not* talking about one's past life.[12]

The meaning of poverty was discussed. Again, she felt on the outside of the majority opinion. "I didn't agree with the notion of deciding what you need to live. I think we should live like the lower class and give witness to our poverty."

Some of the recently arrived sisters from New Mexico found Wisconsin winters too difficult, and they transferred to warmer places. It seems life had not really settled down in Pewaukee. She writes in a single entry that several sisters were taking leaves of absence, but that the warblers and white throated sparrows were still around. Nature was keeping things balanced it seemed to her. Scenes around the lake still spoke to her heart. "Today, yellow leaves against light blue water. A flock of wild geese went over. Sr. Elizabeth came back."[13]

Change was harder to assimilate than she expected. Her dreams reveal her sense of lostness, her need to be settled. In one dream she is in a city, going back and forth from a train station, seeking someone in authority, but also looking for a lost box full of letters. She finds the box, but it is in disorder. Fr. Thomas Kilduff is in the dream, and she tries to talk to him but he is busy. She sees a large building with many Carmelites and wonders if she can stay there.

In another dream she is searching for a place to live "and it seemed it was a room I was looking for, not a house. There was a terrible storm coming. I went into our typing room next to my cell and I saw that there was not only a storm but a lovely sunset outside, over the lake. I think I was still unsettled that I hadn't found a room."

But in fact she did settle. Her work helped. (In her dream it is in the typing room where she is able to see the beautiful sunset.)

The 1974 summer retreat with the prophets helped, too, as did a review of her old journals. She read through her own commentaries on the troubles of the sixties. Time has provided a different perspective. "Could it have been that bad? After about the middle of the book (the journal) I either reformed or just gave up confessing my weakness." About the present she writes, "Now I keep climbing over the ruins and going on. If I didn't have Jesus as repairer of fences I'd give up." A poem, "Repairer of Fences," she had written twenty years earlier seemed poignantly apt for this moment.

I am alone in the dark, and I am thinking
what darkness would be mine if I could see
the ruin I wrought in every place I wandered
and if I could not be
aware of One who follows after me.
Whom do I love, O God, when I love Thee?
The great Undoer who has torn apart
the walls I built against a human heart,
the Mender who has sewn together the hedges
through which I broke when I went seeking ill,
the Love who follows and forgives me still.
Fumbler and fool that I am, with things around me
of fragile make like souls, how I am blessed
to hear behind me footsteps of a Savior!
I sing to the east; I sing to the west:
God is my repairer of fences, turning my paths into
rest. (14)

A determination to turn her thoughts to benefits for others and "forget myself," helped. She sees her mother in this renewed outlook, and she thinks about what Fr. Dan Berrigan was supposed to have said—"probably a misquote but I love it," she writes, namely "When Christ comes I want to be where He expects to find me." She was convinced more than ever that the place where she would be found was Pewaukee. So much living had gone on there. Later she would quote James Stevens to explain it all: "The music of what happens is the most beautiful music of all."[14]

Her seventieth birthday (February 7, 1975) was quiet. She read Butler's *Lives of the Saints* (or portions of it.) A week later the nuns gave a surprise birthday party for her. There was a special dinner prepared by Sr. Mary Bernadette, decorations on the walls, and gifts from everyone: a new habit, a jacket, a toothbrush, garden gloves, stationery, Peptobysmol, and three pairs of shoes, one of them high-heels. She later dreamed of the high-heels, (in her dream she had bought them). The straps were unfastened and she thought, "Why did I buy them? I deserve this!" She would never get over her longing for the old sandals and all they symbolized. But she was well practiced by now in either climbing over ruins, or moving on to the next threshold. Change may have been hard for her but it was not impossible. Long ago she chose the difficult path, with careful deliberation.

Death came back again to Jessica in the decade of the seventies. Allie Keegan died in 1974, as did Clifford Laube. Her brother John in 1977. Tony Pegis in 1978 (on May 13th, his wife, Jessie's birthday). Jessie had moved to a retirement home in Toronto. One of the Pewaukee nuns who had left the monastery and was now living in Toronto wrote to Jessica about her friend. She said that in many ways "It was as if Tony were still there." Jessie died in 1988, six months before Jessica.

On December 26, 1979, Sister Lucille was gone. Fifty-four years before Jessica had written to "Dearest Sister Lucille" a letter about death. Sister Lucille had lost someone close to her at that time and Jessica, a young woman of twenty, wrote a letter of consolation.

> It's so very difficult to watch our loved ones go out the door into Eternity, leaving us so utterly alone. We ought rather to rejoice that God has called home His child into everlasting ultimate happiness . . .

The letter continues with prayers and the "gift of my heart . . . because I love you—and I want you to be happy forever and forever. Lovingly, Jessica."[15] This was a loss on a par with her mother's death. Her early muse no longer walked the earth. By this time, however, she was as practiced in loss as she was in climbing over the ruins.

The story of these years of sorrow, confusion and spiritual survival (and more—of wisdom and integration) appears in the poem, "Wanderer," first published in *Commonweal* in 1979. She claims the Scivias of St. Hildegarde as her inspiration, but it is reflective of her own life, as well.

Where did I dwell? I dwelt in the shadow of death,
as did a mystic anciently aver.
Where did I walk? I walked on the primitive
pathway of error, was a child of earth
(and down the years my speech betrayed by birth).
What did I hold for ease against my breast?
The flimsy comfort of a wanderer
for whom there is no rest.

Two nestlings vied for life in me: I fed
the greedy one whose talent was to beg
(no none had warned me of the cowbird's egg).
I let the little one grow thin and pale
and put a blame on life that she was frail.

How did I ever come then to the light?
How did I ever, blind with self, discover
the small strict pathway to this shining place.
I who betrayed the truth over and over,
and let a tangle of dark woods surround me?
simple the answer lies: down cliffs of pain,
through swamps and desert, thicket and terrain,
oh, Someone came and found me. (124)

Found, she continued on her strict pathway. In 1983 there were only eight members of the community, but she seemed content with whatever the future might hold. She wrote to a cousin, a Dominican priest then in Africa, that "It would not take much to dissolve us . . . but God will take care of all His people, we can be sure."[16]

Another book was in preparation, a collection of sixty-one poems, taking its title from the first poem, *The House At Rest.* Most of the poems in the collection had been published elsewhere, but this poem was new. Students of Carl Jung may see in it the symbols of the human personality, and indeed, Jessica's own tracking of her dreams reveals the centrality of "the house" in her personal symbolism. She begins the poem, (and, perhaps the prologue to the finale) with lines from John of the Cross:

On a dark night
Kindled in love with yearnings—
Oh, happy chance!—

I went forth unobserved,
My house now being at rest.

How does one hush one's house,
each proud possessive wall, each sighing rafter,
the rooms made restless with remembered laughter
or wounding echoes, the permissive doors,
the stairs that vacillate from up to down,
windows that bring in color or event
from countryside or town,
oppressive ceilings and complaining floors?

The house must first of all accept the night.
Let it erase the walls and their display,
impoverish the rooms till they are filled
with humble silences; let clocks be stilled
and all the selfish urgencies of day.

Midnight is not the time to greet a guest,
Caution the doors against both foes and friends,
and try to make the windows understand
their unimportance when the daylight ends.
Persuade the stairs to patience, and deny
the passages their aimless to and fro.
Virtue it is that puts a house at rest.
How well repaid that tenant is, how blest
who, when the call is heard,
is free to take his kindled heart and go. (122)

She consulted with Sister Eileen Surles of the Cenacle, her friend of many years, about the manuscript. With a recent rejection from *America*—"the poems were more statements . . . telling the reader how he or she should feel or think"—her confidence was shaken. Eileen replied that the *America* critic should not be considered the final criterion for judging poetry.

Jessica sought Macmillan as a publisher for the new volume. They were not interested in a volume of poetry at that time. The nuns of Pewaukee urged her to prepare the manuscript for publication by their own monastery, a risk they were all willing to take. Jessica began work with the assistance of one of the nuns. She acquired an additional workroom and a new desk as a result. She spent one joyful day arranging her new space. (From that time until her death she had three rooms: her cell and two workrooms.) *The House at Rest* was released in 1984. Jessica Powers was seventy-nine years of age.

Letter after letter came with the publication of *The House at Rest.* People wrote that they had read Jessica Powers a quarter of a century before, were deeply affected then, and wondered what had become of her. They rejoiced that she was still creating such stirring lyrics. From Italy and Scotland and China as well as throughout the United States came words of appreciation. The sisters of Pewaukee were kept unexpectedly busy filling orders. The book went into second and third printings. First-time readers discovered Jessica Powers. In many ways, her house was at rest, finally.

Both old and new readers were anxious for a complete collection of the poetry of Jessica Powers. Sensing that Jessica's health was failing Sister Regina Siegfried, A.S.C., a friend of twenty years and an Emily Dickinson scholar, and Bishop Robert Morneau, an author, lecturer, and retreat leader, noted for his use of literature in ministry, began an extensive collection of her poetry. Jessica herself was key in the selection and assemblage of the poems, a process that spanned several years. Her osteoporosis worsened during this period causing a large hump on her back. Sleeping was extremely difficult, and the pressure also interfered with her breathing. Her appetite all but disappeared.

She stayed involved in the final editing during the spring and summer of 1988. Sitting at a work table with pages spread before her, she worked with the bishop and with Sister Regina reviewing every poem. The final editing session was a hot July day.

* * * * * * * * *

"Discard the preachy ones," she says, *America's* more recent comments fresh still in her memory.

The poem "Human Winter" survives the cut, and she hastens to explain its origins. Although it was published after she was in Carmel, it is about a New York group of women who were "blasting" another woman absent that day. She wrote the poem to purge herself.

She talks of a long-ago decision to consciously write religious poetry, afraid of the cynicism just beneath the surface of modern poetry. (She was more alarmed than pleased when *Harper's* published two of her poems in 1940).

She notices a computer error, something small, but an error nonetheless. "I'm very exacting as far as poetry goes," she says, and adds, "But I'm a sloppy worker when it comes to housework. Hurricane Hilda I am."

The work continues even though she has trouble breathing from time to time. Every poem is combed, approved. But times have changed. Maps have changed. Are there five continents or six she wants to know?

There are asides. She confides that growing older shocks her. "I used to write about pain and dying before I really knew what they were." On the other hand she admits to being fearful, "that I don't go out after suffering like the saints." Still, she remembers when President Carter asked that the heat be lowered to 65 degrees as an energy conservation measure. She liked the idea of a penance *not* of one's asking. (She liked, too, the president's straightforwardness.)

She brings up the subject of persons with AIDS. "I think they are very close to Christ. Not only because of their suffering, but because they are shunned by some."

She speaks of heaven as an eternal discovery. "We'll be with the whole human race and we'll learn their stories."

She offers this. "As you progress in the spiritual life you progress in ordinary living." That's another way of stating the Eugene Bianchi principle that the elders who are integrating their lives are still very much involved with life.

The editing is almost complete. She smiles and says "Let's go to a far island where people don't know our language and we don't know theirs. We'll have brown bag lunches everyday. . ."[17] At age eighty-three Jessica Powers was about to set out again for a place she had never been, strains of winter music in the air.

* * * * * * * * *

The Homecoming

The spirit, newly freed from earth,
is all amazed at the surprise
of her belonging: suddenly
as native to eternity
to see herself, to realize
the heritage that lets her be
at home where all this glory lies.

By naught foretold could she have guessed
such welcome home: the robe, the ring,
music and endless banqueting,
these people hers; this place of rest
known, as of long remembering
herself a child of God and pressed
with warm endearments to His breast. (53)

Postlude

The monastery on the hillside of Pewaukee Lake continues the Carmelite rhythms of prayer and work, of solitude and community, home to a small community of sisters. The spirit of Jessica Powers is evident. At Advent the sisters remember her love for Isaiah and how she would counsel the wisdom and grace of entering deeply into the liturgical season of expectance. The sisters are mindful of the phrase "to enter deeply," for that is what their life is about: depth. There is a sense of newness these days in the monastery.

One sister is learning the organ, and now music is always a possibility. The novice director has been busy about shaping a formation program. A new member of the community is cataloguing the five-thousand plus library. Another tends the garden in summer, and concentrates on her needlepoint in winter. Sr. Mary Bernadette, who died some months after Jessica, would approve of the new sister-cook who transforms the humblest offerings into delicious healthy "feasts." A novice recently consecrated her life to God; that would give joy to Jessica.

Other women come to see what life inside the monastery is all about, to ascertain if God is inviting them to abide there beside the lake. A new prioress, young and full of hope, has been elected. Together the small but growing community has worked on their particular application of the rule of life; they think Jessica, who valued tradition but not rigidity, would like the interpretation. There is a discernible strong pulse in the community.

The sisters, like generations of Carmelites before them, pray unceasingly for those whose lives touch theirs, and for the countless others whom they do not know and who have never heard of them. They quote from a poem of Jessica's. "Love is a simple plant like Creeping Charlie; once it takes root its talent is to spread" ("My Heart Ran Forth," 45).

They pray that in the spreading of Christ's love in individual lives, all the world will be filled with enduring love.[1]

Sunsets still explode across the Wisconsin skies. As always, birds in great variety inhabit the trees. Snow remains a fact of winter life. The lantern still burns in the Mother of God Carmel, a small, steady light on the hill beside Pewaukee Lake.

Notes

Prelude

1. Jessica Powers, *Selected Poetry of Jessica Powers,* ed. Regina Siegfried A.S.C., and Robert F. Morneau (Kansas City, Missouri: Sheed & Ward, 1989). Hereafter, citations from *Selected Poetry of Jessica Powers* have been abbreviated to parenthetical page references.
2. Jessica Powers, "The Variable Heart." This version is in *The House of Splendor* (New York: Cosmopolitan Science and Art Service Co., Inc., 1946), 36.
3. Rainer Maria Rilke, *Letters to a Young Poet,* trans. M.D. Herter Norton (New York: W.W. Norton & Co., Inc., 1962), 53.
4. Jessica Powers, "The Little Nation" in *The Place Of Splendor,* 29.
5. Willa Cather, *Willa Cather on Writing* (Lincoln and London, University of Nebraska Press, 1988), 13.
6. Robert Morneau, *Mantras from a Poet* (Kansas City, Sheed and Ward, 1991).
7. See Marcia Ann Kappes, *Track of the Mystic*: Carmelite Influence on the American Poet Jessica Powers (1905-1988); doctoral dissertation St. Louis University.
8. Jacob Weisberg, "Rhymed Ambition" in *The Washington Post Magazine,* January 19, 1992.

   This article focused on Joseph Brodsky, the current poet laureate of the United States, is an appeal to return poetry to the mainstream of American life. Also see Dana Gioia, "Can Poetry Matter" in *The Atlantic Monthly*, May 1991, 94-106. Gioia points out that poets today are writing for other poets, and for academicians, thus removing poetry from the center of literary life.
9. See Bernard McGarty, "An Emily Dickinson from Juneau County" in *Times Review*, June 24, 1982. (*The Times Review* is a weekly publication of the diocese of La Crosse, Wisconsin.)
10. Konrad Lorenz, *The Year Of The Greylag Goose* (New York: Harcourt Brace Jovanovich, 1978), 191.

PART ONE: WISCONSIN

1. This information is from *Wisconsin, A Guide to the Badger State,* compiled by Workers of the Writers' Program of the WPA in Wisconsin. (New York: Hastings House Publishers, 1976).
2. Quoted in Meridel Le Sueur, *North Star Country* (New York: Buell, Sloan and Pearce, 1945), 16.

Chapter One

1. May Sarton, *Writings on Writing* (Orono, Maine: Pucherbrush Press, 1980), 40.
2. Jessica Powers's notebooks in the Marquette University archives, Milwaukee, Wisconsin.
3. Allen Ginsberg, "Meditation and Poetics" in *Spiritual Quests,* ed. William Zinsser (Boston: Houghton Mifflin Company).
4. Jessica Powers's correspondence with Christopher Powell, Marquette University archives.
5. Quoted in Robert Morneau's Introduction to *Selected Poetry of Jessica Powers,* xvii.

Chapter Two

1. Information about Catherine Hyde is from family papers and from interviews with Jessica Powers, 1986-1988.
2. Information about the Powers family is taken from family records in the Marquette University archives. Information about Cat Tail Valley is from articles prepared by William Walsh for the Juneau County historical society, and from author interviews with William Walsh.
3. The James Trainer letter and other information about the Trainer family were supplied by Doris Trainer Scully of Lyndon Station, who also provided historical background about Lyndon Station.
4. A. M. Allchin, *The World is a Wedding* (New York, Oxford University Press, 1978), 19.

Chapter Three

1. Taped group interview at St. Patrick's rectory, October, 1988.
2. Author interview with Philip Quinn of Mauston, November, 1989.
3. Notes in Jessica Powers's journal. Marquette University archives.
4. Taped interview with Mary Walsh, November, 1989.

Chapter Four

1. An account of this renaming can be found in an article by Rev. Bernard McGarty in the *Times Review* June 14, 1984. The *Times Review* is a weekly published by the Diocese of La-Crosse in Wisconsin.
2. Jessica Powers's journal, Marquette University archives.
3. Information about Minnie Saunders and the school boarders is from a taped group interview with friends and relatives of Jessica Powers, October 1988, in St. Patrick's rectory, Mauston, Wisconsin.
4. May Sarton, *Writings on Writing*, 39.
5. *Ibid.*, 42.
6. *Ibid.*, 42-43.
7. An unpublished poem of Jessica Powers in a private collection of Mary Walsh of Mauston.
8. This childhood writing is preserved in the archives of the Mother of God Carmel in Pewaukee, Wisconsin.
9. May Sarton, *Writings On Writing*, 43.
10. Jessica Powers, "The Saints Come Here To Worship" in a private collection of Mary Walsh of Mauston.
11. Patricia Hampl, *A Romantic Education* (Boston: Houghton Mifflin Company, 1981), 17.
12. Taped interview with Jessica Powers, July 1988.
13. Carolyn Heilbrun, *Writing A Woman's Life,* (New York/London: W.W. Norton, 1988), 53.

Chapter Five

1. This information on Milwaukee is from *Wisconsin: A Guide to the Badger State*, compiled by Workers of the Writers' Program of the Work Projects Administration in the state of Wisconsin, (New York: Hastings House, 1941; republished in 1976), 240-248.
2. There is no indication that this poem was published elsewhere. Jessica Powers's original rendering of the last lines of the poem was changed to "grandmother's eyes."
3. All of the information about the Marquette University School of Journalism 1922-1923 is from the University Bulletin of those years.
4. "To Aimee" is in the private collection of Mary Walsh of Mauston, Wisconsin.
5. "The Cat-Tails," an unpublished poem written in 1923 or 1924; Marquette University archives.
6. Taped interview in 1987.

7. "Michigan Boulevard," the first of two poems by this title, unpublished. The second version, first published in 1932 in the *Chicago Tribune* can be found in *Selected Poetry of Jessica Powers,* 82.
8. Allen Ginzberg writes that poetry is rarely "just poetry"; it is more fascination with a phenomenal universe; furthermore, "classical poetry is a probe into the nature of reality." "Meditations and Poetics" in *Spiritual Quests: The Art and Craft of Writing,* William Zinsser, ed. (Boston: Houghton Mifflin Company, 1988). This seems particularly apt for Jessica Powers whose life was given to probing, exploring, singing the wonders of the natural universe.
9. Blackfriars Theater was a Dominican supported theatrical enterprise in New York City where Urban Nagle, a Dominican, played a central role in management and production.
10. "Church of Our Lady of Sorrows, Chicago" in *The Lantern Burns,* limited edition by Monastine Press (New York, 1939), 34.
11. Jessica Powers, *The Lantern Burns* (New York: Monastine Press, 1939).
12. August Flint and William H. Welch, *The Principles and Practice of Medicine,* Fifth edition, 1888.
13. Susan Sontag, *Illness As Metaphor* (New York: Farrar, Straus, Giroux, 1977).

Chapter Six

1. *American Poetry Magazine* was begun in 1919 by Clara Catherine Prince. The magazine continued for forty-five years.
2. Interview with Mary Walsh of Mauston, Wisconsin.
3. *Ibid.*
4. *Ibid.*
5. Obituary supplied by William Walsh of Mauston, Wisconsin.
6. Jessica Powers, "The Dead," unpublished poem in Marquette University archives.
7. The Sterling North assessment is in a Jessica Powers letter to August Derleth (May 14, 1936) in response to his request to include some of her verses in a Wisconsin anthology Derleth was preparing. The letter is in the August Derleth Papers (Box 40) at the State Historical Society of Wisconsin.
8. For example, poems of James Whitcomb Riley were copied in calligraphy.
9. Jessica Powers-Christopher Powell correspondence, letter #3, Marquette University archives.

10. Powers-Powell correspondence, letter #3 and #4, Marquette University archives.
11. See Willa Cather "Escapism" *Willa Cather On Writing* (Lincoln/London: University of Nebraska Press, 1988), 27-28.
12. Jessica Powers correspondence with Sr. Lucille, OP; in the Edgewood College archives, Racine, Wisconsin.
13. Powers-Powell correspondence, letter #4, Marquette University archives. (Chalk marks were placed on fences by tramps indicating a house house or a farm was a good place for food.)
14. Interview with Jessica Powers, September 11, 1985.
15. Powers-Powell correspondence, letter #4, Marquette University archives.
16. Powers-Powell correspondence, letter #6, Marquette University archives.
17. Jessica Powers, "Michael," published in *The Carillion*; see notebooks in Marquette University archives.
18. Jessica Powers correspondence with Ruth Mary Fox in Edgewood College archives.
19. Powers-Powell correspondence, letter #5, Marquette University archives.
20. Powers-Powell correspondence, letter #7, Marquette University archives.
21. "They Tell Me," an unpublished poem in Jessica Powers files, Marquette University archives.
22. Kate Farrell, *Art and Love* (New York: The Metropolitan Museum of Art, Little Brown and Company), 11.
23. Interview with Jessica Powers, September 1986.
24. Powers-Powell correspondence, letter #13, Marquette University archives.
25. See Chapter One.

PART TWO: NEW YORK

1. Information about early New York is from Jerry E. Patterson, *A History Illustrated from the Collections of the Museum of the City of New York* (New York: Harry N. Abrams, Inc., 1978).

Chapter Seven

1. Transcript of interview with Jessica Powers conducted by Bishop Robert Morneau and Sr. Regina Siegfried.
2. Jessica Powers's naming of and devotion to her guardian angel can be found in the notebooks, journals and scrapbook she kept for many years. Marquette University archives. She also spoke about her angel in several interviews with the author.

3. This summary of the world's political status at this time is based on information found in *An Encyclopedia of World History,* ed. William L. Langer (Boston: Houghton-Mifflin Co., 1968.)
4. Margaret Mary Rehr, *Catholic Intellectual Life in America* in the series *The Bicentennial History of the Catholic Church in America*, Christopher J. Kauffman, general editor, (New York: Macmillan Publishing Company, 1989), 123.
5. Author interview with Mary Walsh.
6. Letter to Alice Keegan of Mauston, Wisconsin; in the Marquette University archives.
7. Author interview with Sr. Eileen Surles, R.C.

Chapter Eight

1. In Catholic tradition Holy Years are usually celebrated every twenty-five years. Announced by the Pope, they signal a time of forgiveness, remembrance and renewal. The practice can be traced to the Jewish custom of jubilee years.
2. Wilfrid Sheed, *Frank And Maisie: A Memoir With Parents* (New York: Simon and Schuster, 1985), 125. Most of the information about Frank Sheed and Maisie Ward is taken from this memoir.
3. Note to Dorothy Day from Jessica Powers; archives, Marquette University.
4. "Rag Man" appeared in the July 1942 issue of *The Catholic Worker* and was reprinted in *The Place Of Splendor* (New York: Cosmopolitan Science and Art Service Co., Inc., 1946.), 73. *The Place of Splendor* is a collection of 73 poems, many of which are in the 1989 Sheed and Ward collection, *Selected Poetry of Jessica Powers*; "The Rag Man" is not included.
5. See "Uncommon Women and Others" by Albert Schorsch III in *U.S. Catholic Historian*, 371.
6. See Florence Henderson Davis, "Lay Movements in New York City During the thirties and Forties" in *U.S. Catholic Historian* 9:4 (Fall, 1990) p. 401.
7. Stanley Vishnewski, "She Ain't White and She Ain't Colored," *Restoration.* Memorial edition (February-March, 1986), cited by Florence Henderson Davis in *U.S. Catholic Historian, ibid.*
8. This sketch of Clifford Laube is based on an article in *The New York Sun* (Sept. 13, 1939) and on interviews with his daughter and son-in-law, Genevieve Laube Tully and John Tully, and with his granddaughter, Sr. Magdalene, O.C.D., a cloistered Carmelite.
9. *The New York Sun,* (Sept. 13, 1939), p. 16.

10. Clifford Laube, “Crabapple Trees” in *Crags* (New York: Monastine Press, 1938), 24.
11. Story told by Jessica Powers in interview with author.
12. *The New York Sun*, op. cit.
13. This scene is based on newspaper articles in *The Sunday Call* (Newark, N.J.) and *The New York Sun*, *op. cit.*, and on interviews with Sr. Eileen Surles, RC, and the Laube family as cited above.
14. Correspondence with Christopher Powell; Marquette University archives.
15. Letter to Clifford Laube, supplied by the Laube family.
16. Interview with Sr. Magdalene, O.C.D.
17. Jessica Powers, “Spell Against New York,” unpublished; in Jessica Powers's papers, Marquette University archives.
18. Letter to Clifford Laube, *ibid*.

Chapter Nine

1. William Wordsworth, “Ode: Intimatious of Immortality From Recollections of Early Childhood” in *Immortal Poems of the English Language* ed. Oscar Williams (New York: Washington Square Press, Inc., 1952), 260.
2. Author interview with Sister Eileen Surles, R.C.
3. Jessica Powers's correspondence with Sr. Lucille Massart, letter #C12; archives, Oscar Rennebohm Library, Edgewood College, Madison, WI.
4. *Third* orders are lay persons who live and work in secular settings, but who follow a “rule” or way of life adapted from that of the *first* order (priests) and/or the *second* order (sisters/nuns).
5. Jessica Powers's correspondence with Sister Lucille, letter #C13.
6. Author interview with Sister Eileen Surles, RC.
7. *Ibid.*
8. Jessica Powers's correspondence with Sister Lucille, letter #C13.
9. The poem's title was changed to “To Richard Aged One” when it was published in an article about Jessica Powers's entrance into Carmel. The article appeared in *The Milwaukee Catholic Herald*.
10. The greeting card verses as well as the “Songs of the Seashore” are in the Marquette University archives.
11. Author interview with Sister Eileen Surles, R.C.
12. August Derleth Papers, State Historical Society of Wisconsin, Box 40.

13. See "Place of Hawks" by Jane Eiseley in *Wisconsin Academy Review, A Journal of Wisconsin Culture*, Summer 1991.
14. Introduction to *August Derleth: A Bibliography* by Alison M. Wilson (New Jersey and London: The Scarecrow Press, Inc., 1983).
15. Author interview with Mary Walsh.
16. Publisher's note is on the jacket of the original edition; a private collection of Rev. Daniel Morrissey, O.P., chaplain at Columbia University Medical School, New York.
17. Jessica Powers's correspondence, Marquette University archives.
18. Review of *The Lantern Burns* in *Spirit* 6:5 (Nov. 1939), 152-153.
19. Jessica Powers—Christopher Powell correspondence; letter #16, Marquette University archives.
20. Information about Raymond E.F. Larsson supplied by the curator of the Poetry/Rare Books Collection at the State University of New York at Buffalo.
21. The draft manuscript, with introduction by Raymond Larsson is in the Marquette University archives. The poem "Renunciation" is in *Selected Poetry of Jessica Powers*, 109.
22. Jessica Powers's correspondence with Sister Lucille, Edgewood College Archives.
23. Jessica Powers's correspondence, Marquette University archives.
24. Author interview with Sister Eileen Surles, RC
25. Author interview with Mary Walsh.

PART THREE: CARMEL

1. *The Carmelite Adventure,* volume II, ed., Constance Fitzgerald, O.C.D. (Baltimore, Maryland: Carmelite Sisters, 1990), 4.

Chapter Ten

1. Descriptive details about the original Mother of God Carmel are in a booklet about the monastery available in the Pewaukee monastery.
2. Correspondence held by the sisters at the Pewaukee carmel.
3. Profession is the taking of three vows: poverty, chastity and obedience. Prior to renewal, the Carmelites continued to wear their white veils and stayed in the novitiate for three more years, until *final* profession. At that time one received the black veil, only then becoming a Chapter member: i.e., a *voting* member.
4. Written commentary by Sister Eileen Surles, RC.
5. Jessica Powers—Mother Paula correspondence; Pewaukee carmel.

6. Written commentary by Sister Eileen Surles, RC.
7. Information about Washington, D.C. on December 7, 1941 is taken from two articles, one by Haynes Johnson, the other by Shirley Povich in a *Washington Post* special article, "50 Years After Pearl Harbor," December 7, 1991.
8. Jessica Powers—Alice Keegan correspondence; and Jessica Powers—Mary Walsh correspondence; Marquette University archives.
9. Sr. Therese Lentfoehr, "Jessica Takes The Veil" in *Give Joan A Sword* (New York: Macmillan Co., 1944), 71.
10. Author interview with people of Mauston; October 1988.
11. Author interview with Jessica Powers.
12. Aelred of Rievaulx, *Spiritual Friendship,* trans. Mary Eugenia Luker, SSND, (Kalamazoo, Michigan: Cistercian Publications, 1977), 105.
13. Author interview with Jessica Powers.
14. Powers, "This Generation of War" in *The Place of Splendor* (New York: Cosmopolitan Science and Art Service Company, Inc., 1946), 34.
15. John Brunini, "Of Love and Peace" in *Spirit,* 14:2 (May, 1947):57-58.
16. Jessica Powers—John Moffit correspondence; Marquette University archives.
17. Taped editing session, July 1988, in the Pewaukee carmel.
18. Thomas P. McDonnell, "The Nun As Poet" in *Spirit* 26:1 (March, 1959):20-26.
19. Taped editing session, July 1988, in the Pewaukee, carmel.
20. Detailed descriptions of Carmelite customs can be found in the archives of the Baltimore Carmelite monastery.
21. Jessica Powers—Sr. Lucille Massart correspondence, Edgewood College.
22. *Ibid.*

Chapter Eleven

1. Author interview with the nuns of the Elysburg Carmel in Pennsylvania.
2. Author telephone interview with Msgr. Francis Dougherty, October, 1988.
3. Author interviews with several nuns, Carmelites and others.
4. Journals of Jessica Powers, Marquette University archives.
5. Conversation at the Jessica Powers symposium, Marquette University, August 26, 1989.

6. Carmelite biographical piece of Sr. Miriam of the Holy Spirit, prepared at the time of her death in 1988.
7. Journals of Jessica Powers, Marquette University archives.
8. Jessica Powers—Ruth Mary Fox correspondence; Edgemont College archives, Madison, Wisconsin.
9. Sister Therese Lentfoehr, "Ballad at Pentecost," *America*, June 30, 1962, 441.
10. On December 1, 1955, Rosa Parks, an African American Alabama woman refused to move to the back of the bus, according to the custom of the segregated South. For a moving account of the Civil Rights Movement see Taylor Branch, *Parting the Waters* (New York: Simon and Schuster, 1988).
11. Journals of Jessica Powers, Marquette University archives.
12. *Ibid.*
13. The information about the difficulties in the Mother of God Carmel was provided by people who lived there during that period and by other Carmelite nuns.
14. Author interview with Sister Margaret Ellen Traxler, S.S.N.D.
15. Author interview with Sister Desiree O.C.D., now deceased.
16. Jessica Powers—Alice Keegan correspondence, Marquette University archives.
17. The journeys to San Diego and Reno are based on journal entries: Marquette University archives.
18. May Sarton, *A World of Light,* 108.

Chapter Twelve

1. Florida Scott-Maxwell, *The Measure of My Days* (New York: Knopf, 1968).
2. William Butler Yeats, "A Prayer for Old Age" in *W.B. Yeats, The Poems*, ed. Richard J. Finneran (New York: Macmillan Publishing Company, 1983), 282-283.
3. For a discussion of the positive and negative aspects of the later years see Eugene Bianchi, *Aging As A Spiritual Journey*, (New York: Crossroad, 1982).
4. See Pierre Teilhard de Chardin, *The Divine Milieu* (New York: Harper & Row, 1960); quoted in Eugene Bianchi, *Aging As A Spiritual Journey.*
5. Charles Kuralt, program notes for compact disc, "Horowitz in Moscow," Deutche Grammophon.
6. T.S. Eliot, "Four Quartets" (New York: Harvest Books, 1943), 59.
7. Journals of Jessica Powers, Marquette University archives.
8. *Ibid.*

9. Sr. Miriam, OCD, "Up the High Mountain," *Discalced Carmelite Proper Offices,* (New York: Catholic Book Publishing Company, 1980), 218.
10. Correspondence between Sr. Miriam, OCD and Fr. John Sullivan, OCD. Private collection (John Sullivan, O.C.D.)
11. Journals of Jessica Powers, Marquette University archives.
12. *Ibid.*
13. *Ibid.*
14. *Ibid.*
15. Jessica Powers—Sr. Lucille correspondence, Edgemont College, Madison, Wisconsin.
16. Jessica Powers correspondence with Fr. Bede Jogue, O.P., provided by Father Jogue.
17. Final editing session (taped) for *Selected Poetry of Jessica Powers.*

Postlude

1. From the Advent-Christmas letter of the Mother of God Carmel.

Index